APR   2009

WEEKEND SEWING

More Than 40 Projects and Ideas for Inspired Stitching

Heather Ross

PHOTOGRAPHS by John Gruen

STC Craft | A Melanie Falick Book

STEWART, TABORI & CHANG
NEW YORK

For My Sister,
Christine Domino Danner

Published in 2009 by Stewart, Tabori & Chang
An imprint of Harry N. Abrams, Inc.

Text and illustrations copyright © 2009 by Heather Ross
Photographs copyright © 2009 by John Gruen

Library of Congress Cataloging-in-Publication Data

Ross, Heather.
Weekend sewing: More than 40 projects and ideas for inspired stitching / Heather Ross.
p. cm.
"STC Craft/A Melanie Falick book."
ISBN 978-1-58479-675-6
1. Sewing. 2. Clothing and dress. 3. House furnishings. I. Title.

TT705.R67 2008
646.2--dc22

            2008018851

Editor: Melanie Falick
Technical Editor: Christine Timmons
Designer: Brooke Hellewell Reynolds
Production Manager: Jacqueline Poirier

The text of this book was composed in Avenir.
Printed and bound in China.

10 9 8 7 6 5 4 3 2 1

HNA
harry n. abrams, inc.
a subsidiary of La Martinière Groupe

115 West 18th Street
New York, NY 10011
www.hnabooks.com

CONTENTS

INTRODUCTION

As a child, I lived with my mom and twin sister in a one-room schoolhouse in the mountains of Northern Vermont. My daily routine was guided by the light and the seasons because—aside from school—there really was nowhere else to be. Our property was bordered by a rushing river that tumbled into a tall waterfall and ended in a deep and perfect swimming hole. Whenever we could, my sister and I would swim and explore the woods and orchards around our house, but when the long, dark winters drove us inside, we would spend countless hours executing elaborate craft projects.

Both of us learned to sew and knit early, and by the time we were five years old, we were already stitching costumes for our dolls and for one very reluctant but tragically slow-moving tomcat. We created silly costumes for each other, stitched tiny winter coats for the house-gnomes we imagined needing them, and knitted even tinier scarves for blue jays with toothpicks and embroidery floss. I vividly recall the bright spring day I decided to plug in my great-grandmother's mint green Singer sewing machine: Holding my breath, I switched on the little lightbulb and stomped on the foot pedal as hard as I could, both frightened and thrilled by the power I ignited. The moment I saw the perfectly spaced, secure stitches I had made, I was utterly hooked.

As I grew up, I continued to sew, my fascination fueled by the extensive collection of exotic fabrics that my mother, grandmother, and great-grandmother had collected from destinations far and wide: China, Japan, Indonesia, Austria, and Mexico. Heavy silk brocades, kimono fabrics, hand-printed batiks, felted wools, and brightly colored serapes became dresses, coats, costumes, and handbags. By the time I was twelve, I was planning and staging fashion shows for my extended family, and by sixteen, I was running a cottage industry from my kitchen table, making prom dresses and ski suits for my friends and classmates. Oddly, it had never occurred to me that I could choose art as a career. When I went to college, I studied history and law, putting aside sewing and other crafts for a few years to concentrate on a career that would give my life the structure and stability that my childhood lacked. But not long after finishing college, I found myself craving art,

color, and even chaos, and the ideas and projects that filled my mind actually kept me awake at night. I so fondly recalled those long, unscheduled days of sewing and sketching—and that chest of exotic fabrics—that one day I found myself enrolled in folk art classes in San Miguel D'Allende, Mexico, having left my structured life and my wristwatch far behind.

One thing led to another: I moved to northern California after art school and started a line of children's clothing made from my own printed fabrics, featuring ripe apples, wildflowers, inchworms, and house-gnomes—the icons of my childhood. The line was received well, and soon I was running my own company. And wearing a wristwatch. And working on weekends. After almost a decade of this, I was exhausted, and I sold the company. Almost without planning it, the first place I returned to after the ink was dry on the deal was that perfect swimming hole behind that schoolhouse. Amazingly, it was exactly as I had remembered it, as though it had been waiting for me.

These days, I live in New York City, a place that is ruled by the clock. My life as an artist and designer of fabric and clothing requires me to be accessible, punctual, and dressed appropriately (which means shoes, even in the summertime!). From Monday morning through Friday afternoon, my life is generally about deadlines and timelines and bottom lines. Often, it is only during weekends and holidays—and those few work days when I sneak away and play hooky—that I can take time out to sew for pure pleasure. I think of this as "weekend sewing."

Logical as it may seem, for me weekend sewing is not limited to Saturday and Sunday. Rather, I consider it to be any time I am able to immerse myself so fully in the joy of sewing that I lose track of time and even myself, just like I did as a child. It is my hope that with *Weekend Sewing*, this book, I will inspire you to steal some time from your busy life for this simple joy—whether sewing for you is a newfound passion or a lifelong friend.

I filled *Weekend Sewing* with clothing, accessories, and home items that not only can be completed in a weekend, but also seem well suited to weekend style. Some of the projects, like the Quick Garden Gloves, Saturday-Night Silk-Jersey Set, Ruby's Bloomers, or Fat-Quarter Napkins, can be completed in just a few hours. Others, like the Weekend-Away Travel Bag, Trapeze Sundress, or Guest Room Slippers, might take a day or two (How wonderful it is to imagine devoting two whole days to sewing!). And because weekends are often the most fun when they're social, I also included recipes and ideas that might inspire you to invite others in, whether to thread up a machine next to yours and sew the day away, or to share a simple meal, an opinion about hem length, and a good story.

Regardless of when you find your time to sew, I hope you—like me—will find the process of surrounding yourself with fabric, color, pattern, and possibility renewing, and the prospect of emerging from the weekend with a finished project—something both beautiful and useful—immensely satisfying.

On my luckiest of New York City Saturdays, I wander through the farmer's market early in the morning to forage for dinner and cut flowers, stopping at the magazine stand on the way home to scout for fresh ideas. Once home, I will turn to the big wooden cabinet that sits closed and quiet in my living room all week long, and open it to reveal a small world of fabrics, books, sketches, and jars of buttons and trims, all surrounding my ancient but trusty machine. As I sit down and switch on that little lightbulb, my sewing machine comes to life with a scratchy little hum, its motor pausing as though it needs to yawn very largely before greeting me, and then it will be ready to sew, just exactly as I left it, as though it has been waiting for me.

LEFT At the swimming hole, 1978.

BELOW Sewing today.

SETTING UP TO SEW AT HOME

It's important to find a place in your home where you can sew easily. Your machine and other tools need to be readily accessible (you're unlikely to feel inspired to sew if it requires dislodging your machine from the back of a closet or hunting down your pins and needles in the bottom of a drawer). For those of us who live in more cramped quarters, a little ingenuity is required. Featured here are two ideas: At right is a compact, modern "sewing desk" for a hallway or corner, and on page 10 is a more elaborate cabinet that opens up to create an inspiring, functional sewing space.

Sewing Desk

Encouraged by my extremely hip sewing students at Purl Patchwork in New York City, I designed the compact sewing desk for a small apartment, using a storage ottoman to house a tiny vintage Singer Featherweight (though it can also accommodate a larger machine) and other supplies. When not in use, the ottoman slides under the desk, like a chair, or can be moved to other rooms. The desk is expandable and has a small drawer for tools. Its lower surface can hold patterns and large projects when closed and support the sewing machine when open. The upper surface is ideal for working on patterns and cutting; its 35" height is more comfortable to work at while standing. When closed, the desk can double as a table in an entrance or hallway.

ABOVE The ottoman opens to store extra fabric, notions and even a spare machine.

LEFT When expanded, the desk becomes an ideal sewing station, with room to hold notions, work on patterns, cut, and sew.

IRONING BOARD

Hangs to save space. The iron can fit inside the ottoman when not in use.

FABRIC-COVERED BOARD

A wall-mounted inspiration board filled with magazine clippings and fabric swatches can be a wonderful focal point for a sewing area and can help you develop your ideas. It's also a handy spot for trims, larger tools, pattern pieces, and other items.

EXPANDABLE DESK

The front rolls out to create more work surface for sewing or cutting patterns. And there's a small drawer for tools you need close at hand.

OTTOMAN

A comfy chair to sit on, but also extra storage to hold your machine, iron, notions, and/or fabric when not in use.

CORK BOARD
Lining one of the doors with a sheet of thick cork gives you an instant inspiration board.

IRONING BOARD
A board that hangs over your sewing cabinet door can save you time and space.

PULLOUT SHELVES
Computer desks are perfect for sewing. Use the pullout desk for your workspace, and store your machine below when not in use.

Sewing Cabinet

This cabinet-style sewing area is meant to provide a haven of sorts. There is something magical about being able to shutter a secret creative space while you go about your work week, knowing that it is waiting exactly as you left it, ready to come back to life as soon as time allows. I also like that the doors keep out children and significant others, which is perfect for a sewing area that must coexist in a room with toys and flat-screen televisions (to counter the latter, I suggest headphones). I found the cabinet shown here used online for $125, but similar cabinets—sometimes called computer armoires—are easy to source these days. They have a slide-out surface meant to hold a keyboard (or sewing machine) and sometimes another lower slide-out shelf to hold a CPU (which, coincidentally, is the perfect size for a sewing machine). I painted my cabinet a leafy green inside and out, covered the inside of one door with thick cork, and filled it with everything I need for a weekend of sewing.

ANOTHER IDEA

For at least the last ten years I have been on the hunt for the perfect old sewing machine housed in its own cabinet with an extendable tabletop. These sewing cabinets were very popular for decades, for good reason. When closed, they look like and can serve as a small side table, with the sewing machine held upside down inside the cabinet and out of sight. When open, they provide ample space for sewing. My plan is to paint the traditional cabinet a glossy lacquered red (or maybe hot pink) and find the perfect sconce to hang above it, creating a hidden sewing station fit for the chicest of corners. Stay tuned!

LEFT With the doors closed, the cabinet hides your sewing space while keeping tools and notions safely hidden from children and pets.

Chapter 1
HOME AND AWAY

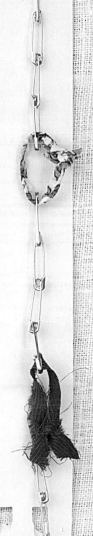

EVERYTHING TOTE

This bag is perfect for weekends and weekdays, with an expanding shape that can hold an unexpectedly large cache of paperwork, groceries, workout gear, books, etc., and wide straps that stay in place on the shoulder.

Finished Dimensions

Approximately 24" x 13" x 8"

Materials

½ yard of heavyweight woven fabric (for tote)

½ yard of lightweight fabric (for lining)

All-purpose thread to match fabric

Water-soluble fabric-marking pen

Everything Tote pattern (see pullout pattern sheet at back of book)

Choosing Fabric

Use a fabric with lots of body for the outside (I like denim or canvas), and be sure to wash everything before you start sewing so that you'll be able to wash your bag afterwards without worrying about shrinkage.

Sewing Instructions

❶ Lay Out and Cut Pattern

Trace (see page 149) the pattern, and cut it out. Then lay out the pattern pieces as shown in the cutting diagram on page 16. From the tote-bag fabric, you'll cut 1 Tote Body, 1 Pocket, 2 Bindings, and 2 Handles. From the lining fabric, you'll cut 1 Tote Lining, 2 Binding Linings, and 2 Handle Linings. Use the water-soluble fabric-marking pen to transfer the points on each side of the Tote Body pattern between which you'll baste in Step 6.

❷ Finish Pocket's Edges

Turn and press all four sides of the Pocket ¼" to the wrong side. Then turn and press the top edge again ½" to the wrong side, and topstitch this edge in place, backstitching (see page 153) at the beginning and end of the seam.

❸ Attach Pocket

Center the Pocket on the right side of one Tote Lining piece 2" from the top edge. Sew around the sides and bottom edge with ⅜" seam, backstitching at the beginning and end of the seam. Then divide the Pocket into two compartments (the small one will hold your cell phone) by sewing straight up from the bottom edge, 3½" from the right edge, backstitching at the beginning and end of the vertical seam.

❹ Sew Side Seams

Fold the tote with right sides facing and the edges aligned, and sew the side seams with a ⅜" seam. Repeat the process with the Tote Lining.

❺ Create Box Corners

With the tote still wrong side out, "box" each corner by sewing across it diagonally, 1½" from the corner. Do not trim the corners; they will add shape to the bag. Repeat this process with the Tote Lining.

❻ Join Tote and Lining

With the tote turned right side out and the Tote Lining still wrong side out, push the lining into the tote, aligning the side seams, so the lining fits squarely inside the tote.

❶ Lay Out and Cut Pattern

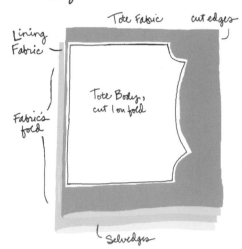

Lining Fabric

Tote Fabric

cut edges

Tote Body, cut 1 on fold

Fabric's fold

Selvedges

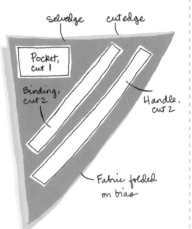

selvedge   cut edge

Pocket, cut 1

Binding, cut 2

Handle, cut 2

Fabric folded on bias

❸ Attach Pocket

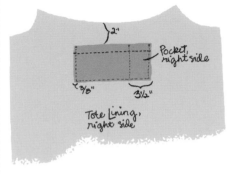

2"

Pocket, right side

3/8"   3½"

Tote Lining, right side

❹-❺ Sew Side Seams and Create Box Corners

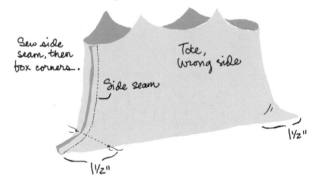

Sew side seam, then box corners.

Side seam

Tote, wrong side

1½"

1½"

❻ Join Tote and Lining

Baste and pull gathers so top edge is 12" wide.

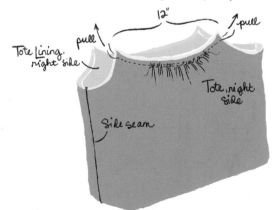

12"

pull   pull

Tote Lining, right side

Tote, right side

Side seam

❼ Bind Tote's Top Edge

Binding Lining right side

Binding, wrong side

¼"

Stitch, turn, and fold.

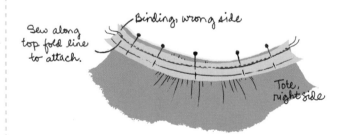

Sew along top fold line to attach.

Binding, wrong side

Tote, right side

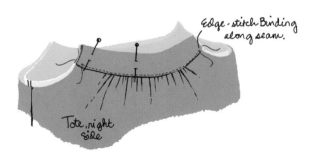

Edge-stitch Binding along seam.

Tote, right side

Using a machine-basting stitch (see page 153), sew along the top edge on each side of the tote and Tote Lining ⅜" from the edge. Leave thread tails at the beginning and end of the seam, and pull the thread tails at each end to create gathers. Adjust the gathers, so the top edge is 12" wide from "peak" to "peak," and knot off the thread tails. Press the gathers flat.

❶ Bind Tote's Top Edges

Prepare Binding strips: To prepare one of the two Binding strips, align the Binding and Binding Lining with the fabrics' right sides together and the edges matched. Join the Binding and lining on both long sides with a ¼" seam, turn the Binding right side out, and press it flat.

Fold and press the Binding in half lengthwise, with the lining sides together. Unfold the Binding, and fold and press each long edge into the center, so the two edges meet at the center fold line. Then press the folded Binding again.

Sew Binding's first edge: Unfold the Binding, and pin one long unfolded edge along one of the tote's top gathered edges, with right sides of the tote and Binding together. Stitch along the Binding's fold 1" from the edge, removing the pins as you sew.

Sew Binding's second edge: Fold the Binding over the tote's gathered edge, and pin the Binding's other folded edge in place. You're going to edge-stitch the pinned edge in place, but to ensure that the edge-stitching looks neat and precise on the tote's right side, I suggest working from the right side. Edge stitch just above the Binding's first seam line, catching the edge on the lining side and removing the pins as you sew.

Repeat the process above with the second Binding to bind the tote's other top edge.

❷ Pin Handles in Place

Prepare first Handle: The handles are made the same way as the binding strips. Align and pin one Handle and one Handle Lining, with right sides together, and join the pair with a ¼" seam along each long side. Turn the Handle right side out, and fold and press it in half lengthwise, with the lining sides together. Unfold the Handle, and fold and press each long edge into the center, so the two edges meet at the center fold line. Then press the folded Handle again.

To hide the raw edges on the Handle's ends, unfold the Handle, and fold and press each short end ¼" to the lining side. Then refold the Handle with the ends tucked in, and press it again.

Pin first Handle: Again unfold the Handle, and pin one long, unfolded edge along one of the tote's top, side edges (see the drawing on page 18), with the tote and Handle right sides together and the Handle's folded short end positioned at one of the tote's side seams. Continue pinning the Handle along the tote's top, side edge, so it covers the end of the sewn Binding, and then let the Handle rise above the tote's top edge.

Pin the Handle's other end at the second side seam, and repeat the pinning process on this side, covering the second end of the sewn Binding strip. Leave unpinned the Handle's folded edges that rise above the tote.

Pin second Handle: Repeat the process above to prepare and pin the tote's second Handle in place, with one exception: Leave the second Handle's ends unfolded. Then align and pin one of the Handle's unfolded ends over the folded end of the first pinned Handle at one side seam. Next align and pin the unfolded long edge of the second Handle along the Tote's other top, side edge, just as you did with the first Handle, pinning the Handle's other unfolded end so it overlaps the folded end of the first Handle.

8-9 Pin and Sew Handles to Tote

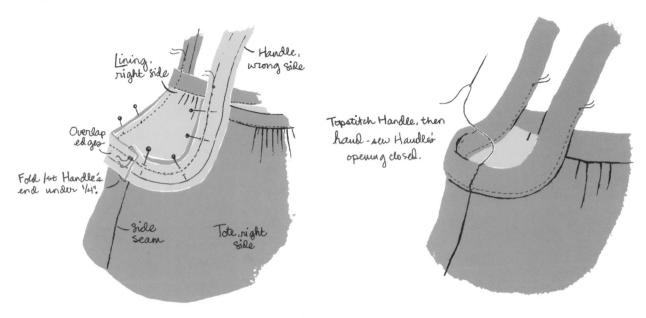

Lining, right side

Handle, wrong side

Overlap edges

Fold 1st Handle's end under 1/4".

side seam

Tote, right side

Topstitch Handle, then hand-sew Handle's opening closed.

---

❾ Sew Handles to Tote

Sew Handles' first long edge: Note that the tote's Handles are stitched to the top, side edges, covering the ends of the Bindings, but are left unstitched in-between. This design makes the Handles more comfortable to carry and also shows off the contrasting lining fabric.

To begin attaching one Handle, sew it to one of the tote's top, side edges, stitching along the Handle's first fold line, stopping 1"-2" past the Binding, and backstitching at the beginning and end of the seam. Then stitch the other end of the Handle in the same way to the second top, side edge. Repeat the process with the second Handle on the tote's other side.

Fold and sew Handles' second long edge: Fold the Handle over the Tote's top, side edge, and pin the Handle's other folded edge in place on the lining side. You'll edge-stitch the Handle's second edge in place from the tote's right side just as you edge-stitched the Binding's second edge in Step 7. Edge-stitch just above the Handle's first seam line, catching the edge on the lining side, removing the pins as you sew, and stopping sewing 1"-2" past the Binding. Be sure to backstitch at the beginning and end of the seam.

Repeat the pinning and sewing process to attach the tote's second Handle. Finally use a slipstitch (see page 155) to hand-sew closed the Handles' opening at each side seam.

Sewing on the Go

One of my favorite ways to spend a free day is to pack up my portable sewing machine (just about any machine is portable, except for the ones that are attached to a table!) and my tools and fabrics and go to a friend's house for some sewing and socializing. I've also heard of groups of friends who share a passion for sewing meeting at a hotel or inn for a marathon weekend of stitching, far from the usual household distractions. I'd love to do that, especially in a town with some really good fabric shops.

Almost any large tote bag or weekend-sized travel bag, including the Everything Tote (shown here), can be retrofitted to hold a sewing machine simply by reinforcing its base with a few layers of stiff cardboard cut to match the shape of the bag's bottom. The zip-up Weekend-Away Travel Bag on page 48 is also perfectly sized to hold a pair of shears and other tools, and its pockets can be filled with spools of thread, bobbins, and pins and needles, both for travel and for stowing at home.

Choosing a lightweight sewing machine is a good idea, whether you plan to travel with it or not, and among new machines there are many options (older machines, typically made of metal, tend to be heavier). A popular choice for quilters and designers who prefer vintage machines and are constantly on the go is the Singer Featherweight model (a pale green one is shown on page 3) which, when fitted snuggly in its carrying case, is ready to hit the road with vintage style, and makes for a lovely centerpiece (and conversation piece) on your hostess's kitchen table.

Finished Dimensions

3 ½" x 6 ½"

Materials

10" square of heavyweight fabric for outside of checkbook (*such as canvas or twill, preferably treated with fabric protector*)

10" square of quilter's cotton for inside of checkbook (*will show very little*)

10" square of contrasting fabric for checkbook's inside pockets (*use heavyweight fabric like for outside of checkbook; will show when checkbook is open*)

Quilter's ruler or straightedge

Point turner

Pinking shears

Embroidery or other small scissors

Spray-on fabric protector (*I like Scotchguard*)

Choosing Fabric

Your fabric should be sturdy enough to survive life at the bottom of your purse, but not so stiff that it's impossible to turn it right side out after sewing the checkbook's seams.

MARKET-RUN CHECKBOOK COVER

This checkbook cover is a great way to use up small pieces of canvas or upholstery fabric, which work especially well if they've been treated to resist stains. I made one of these covers for the daughter of a good friend who was packing up for college (and opening her first bank account!), and tucked a $20 bill inside.

Sewing Instructions

❶ Cut Fabric

After treating your fabric with spray-on fabric protector, following the manufacturer's directions on the label, cut out your pieces, as follows: one 8" x 7 ¼" Cover, one 8" x 7 ¼" Lining, and two 3½" x 7 ¼" Inside Pockets.

❷ Prepare Inside Pockets

Finish the top edge of each Inside Pocket by, first, turning the edge ⅛" to the wrong side, and then pressing the folded edge. Then turn this edge again ⅛" to the wrong side, and press and edge-stitch it.

❸ Layer and Pin Pieces

Lay out your pieces, with the Cover right side up; the two Inside Pockets positioned wrong side up, with their finished top edges placed facing the center of the Lining and their bottom and side edges aligned with the Lining's edges; and the Lining wrong side up and aligned with the edges of the Cover. After laying out and aligning the pieces, pin them in place to keep them from shifting as you work.

❹ Stitch Layers

Starting at one corner, stitch all the way around the checkbook "sandwich" ½" from the raw edges, removing the pins as you come to them and backstitching (see page 153) at the beginning and end of the seam.

❺ Cut Opening in Lining

With the wrong side of the Lining facing you, use small scissors to cut an opening about 3½" long and ½" from the seam on one short side of your lining fabric, being careful to clip through the lining fabric only. In Step 7, you'll turn the checkbook cover right side out through this opening and cover up the opening once you slip a checkbook into the finished cover.

❻ Trim Seams with Pinking Shears

Using your pinking shears, trim the seam allowances on all edges to ¼". (Be sure not to pink too close to the seam line.)

❼ Turn and Shape Cover

Turn the cover right side out by reaching into the cut opening in the lining and pulling each corner through. Use the point turner in each corner to coax the corners to turn out completely. Press the checkbook cover flat.

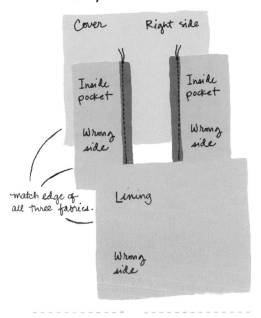

❸ Layer and Pin Pieces

Cover — Right side
Inside pocket — Inside pocket
Wrong side — Wrong side
match edge of all three fabrics.
Lining
Wrong side

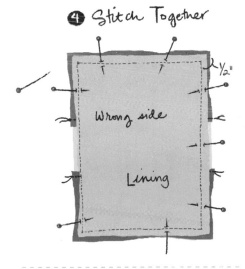

❹ Stitch Together

½"
Wrong side
Lining

5-6 Cut Opening in Lining and Trim Edges

Cutting line — ½"
3½"

SUNDAY-DINNER HOSTESS APRON

My good friend Laura, a brilliant engineer and über-mom, often has friends over for dinner and always has a spare apron waiting. Her kitchen is filled with beautiful pottery, old *Sunset Magazine* cookbooks and clippings, and ingenious tools to make cooking fun. Preparing dinner is a group effort at her house, and there's always a snack and a glass of wine to hold while you stir the paella or an interesting bit of news whispered in your ear while you toss a salad. I've found that once I've tied on one of her aprons, it's difficult to feel like anything less than a part of her family.

Sewing Instructions

① Cut Patterns
Trace (see page 149) the pattern, and cut out the pieces as shown in the cutting diagram on page 24. You will have: 1 Apron Skirt, 1 Waistband, 1 Waistband Facing, 2 Waistband Ties, and 2 Tie Facings.

② Finish Apron's Side Edges
Turn one of the Apron's short edges ⅛" to the wrong side, and press the fold. Turn this edge again ⅛" to the wrong side, and press and edge-stitch (see page 155) the edge in place. Repeat the process on the other short edge.

③ Hem Apron
Hem the Apron's bottom edge by turning it ⅛" to the wrong side and pressing it, then turning it again to the wrong side, this time 5", and pressing and edge-stitching the hem in place.

④ Gather Apron's Top Edge
Gather the Apron's top edge by, first, machine-stitching ¼" from the edge with a long basting stitch (see page 153). Then pull on your needle thread to gather (see page 153) this edge so that it measures approximately 24". Distribute the gathers evenly across the edge, and press the gathers flat.

Finished Dimensions
Apron's length: 20"

Materials

1 yard of woven fabric, preferably in a bold print (or 1⅛ yard fabric *if you don't want contrasting ties*)

⅛ yard of contrasting fabric for ties (*optional*)

Point turner

Water-soluble fabric-marking pen

Sunday-Dinner Hostess Apron pattern (*see pullout pattern sheet at back of book*)

Choosing Fabric

These aprons are lovely made from any woven, mid-weight linen or cotton fabric, especially a fabric with a bold print that will help hide stains. You might also try a contrasting fabric for the waistband or waistband facing for added kick, or you might add a pocket long enough for a tasting spoon.

❶ Cut Patterns

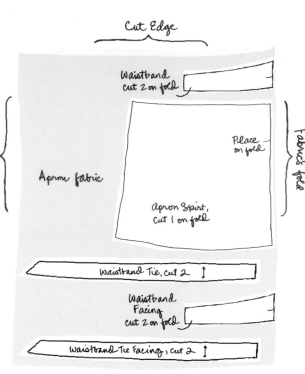

Cut Edge

Waistband
cut 2 on fold

selvedges

Apron fabric

Fabric's fold

Place on fold

Apron Skirt,
Cut 1 on fold

Waistband Tie, cut 2 ↑

Waistband
Facing
cut 2 on fold

Waistband Tie Facing, cut 2 ↑

❷-❸ Finish Apron's Side Edges and Hem Bottom Edge

Apron,
wrong side

⅛" } 5"

❹ Gather Apron's Top Edge

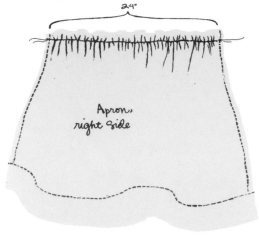

24"

Apron,
right side

❺ Sew Ties to Waistband and Waistband Facing

Waistband, right side

⅜"

Waistband tie,
wrong side

❻-❽ Prepare Waistband, and Join Waistband and Waistband Facing

cut line

⅜"

Wrong side

⅜"

Start sewing above folded edge.

Sew Ties to Waistband and Waistband Facing

With right sides facing, sew Waistband to Waistband Ties, at both ends, with a ⅜" seam. Repeat the process with the Waistband Facing and Tie Facings.

Prepare Waistband

Turn the bottom edge of the Waistband ⅜" to the wrong side, and press but do not sew this edge.

Join Waistband and Waistband Facing

With right sides facing and the edges aligned, sew the Waistband to the Waistband Facing with a ⅜" seam, starting just above the folded edge of one corner and sewing to the same point on the other edge of the Waistband.

Clip Corners and Turn Waistband

Clip the corners of the Ties, and turn the Waistband right side out, using a point turner to push out the corners.

Join Apron and Waistband Facing

With the wrong side of the Apron facing the right side of Waistband Facing, and with the edges matching and the center of the Apron and Waistband aligned, pin the Apron's top edge to the Waistband Facing's bottom edge. Sew the Apron and Waistband Facing together along this edge with a ⅜" seam, removing the pins as you come to them.

Stitch Waistband and Finish

Lay the Apron right side up, fold the Waistband's pressed edge over the joined edges of the Apron and Waistband Facing to conceal them, and press the Waistband and Apron flat. Pin the Waistband's bottom edge in place, and edge-stitch around the entire top and bottom edge of the Waistband and Apron Ties. Press the Apron.

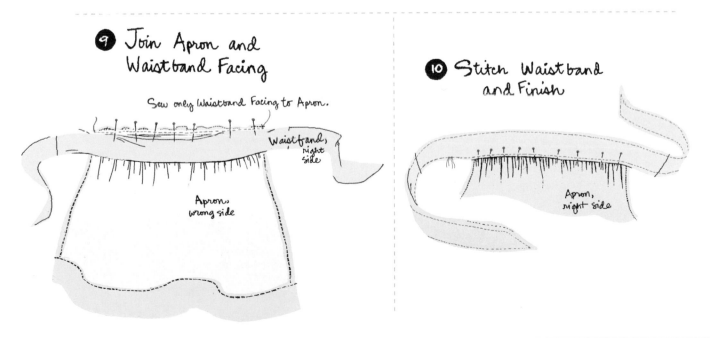

9 Join Apron and Waistband Facing

Sew only Waistband Facing to Apron.

Waistband, right side

Apron, wrong side

10 Stitch Waistband and Finish

Apron, right side

Finished Dimensions

Materials given are for 8 large, 18"-square dinner napkins, with materials for 8 ½"-square cocktail napkins given in parenthesis.

Materials

NOTE: *To make your own fat quarters, follow cutting directions in Introduction at right; then, for cocktail-sized napkins, repeat these steps once, and cut resulting 9" x 11" rectangles or 9" squares.*

16 (4) fat quarters or other lightweight cotton or linen, cut to measure 18" square (9" square)

All-purpose thread (*natural-colored thread blends best with most prints*)

Point turner

Transparent quilter's ruler

Hand-sewing needle

Water-soluble fabric-marking pen

Pinking shears

Choosing Fabric

Quilting cottons, like those I used here, are perfect. But any wide, light- or mid-weight, washable woven fabric will work. All fabrics used for fat quarters should have same fiber content, so they shrink at same rate when washed.

FAT-QUARTER NAPKINS

These napkins are fun for any sewer who loves to mix and match fat quarters, or quarter-yards of fabric that get their name from the way they're cut from the bolt: Instead of dividing the yard of 44"-wide fabric into four narrow quarter-yard strips, a quarter yard is made by cutting the yard in half twice, first lengthwise (making two 18" x 44" cuts) and then across the width (making four 18" x 22" fat quarters).

Preparation

Machine-wash and -dry the fat quarters. Then iron them flat; and, using pinking shears, trim their edges, removing as little fabric as possible. Pair up the fat quarters in combinations you like, and lay the pairs, right side together, on your ironing board. Align the pairs and "true" them (see page 148), so their edges match. Use your steam iron to help shape and square up the fat quarters as much as possible.

Sewing Instructions

① Join Fabric Pairs
With the fat-quarter fabrics' right sides together and with their edges aligned, join each pair with a ¼" seam, starting and ending on one side and leaving a 2 ½" opening in the center of that side.

② Clip Corners and Turn Napkins
Clip the corners to eliminate their bulk so that when you turn the napkin right side out, the corners will form neat points. Turn each napkin right side out, using the point turner to push the corners into shape. Spray each turned napkin with water, and then press it flat.

③ Mark and Topstitch Napkins
Using a transparent quilter's ruler and a water-soluble pen, draw a line parallel to and 1" from each edge. Pin the fabric in place, and topstitch along your marked lines, removing the pins as you sew. Lockstitch (see page 153) the topstitching at the beginning of the seam to secure it: Set the stitch length for zero, and sew several stitches in place; then set the stitch length back to its regular setting to topstitch on your marked lines. At the end of topstitched seam, set the stitch length back to zero, take several stitches in place, remove the napkin from the machine, and clip all thread tails close to the fabric.

④ Hand-Sew Opening Closed
Using a hand-sewing needle, carefully slipstitch (see page 155) the opening closed.

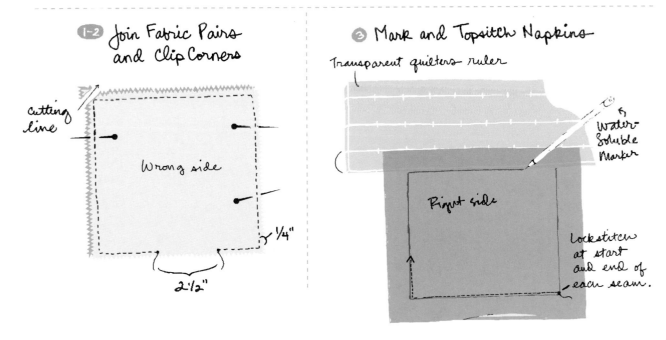

1-2 Join Fabric Pairs and Clip Corners

cutting line

Wrong side

¼"

2½"

③ Mark and Topstitch Napkins

Transparent quilters ruler

Water-Soluble Marker

Right side

Lockstitch at start and end of each seam.

See Materials list below for dimensions that various yardages yield. To make a custom tablecloth, use your tabletop's dimensions and add width and length (typically 12"—or more for more formal look) to allow for overhang.

Materials

Using Irish flax or handkerchief linen, cut one of following:

2 yards of 60"-wide linen *(finished size, approximately 58" x 118")*

1½ yards of 60"-wide linen *(finished size, approximately 58" x 54")*

2 yards of 44"-wide linen *(finished size, approximately 44" x 88")*

1⅛ yards of 44"-wide linen *(finished size, approximately 44" x 45")*

2-3 fat quarters or scraps of mixed, printed fabrics *(for cutting images, florals, or large circles for appliquéing)*

Double-sided fusible interfacing for adhering appliqués

Straightedge ruler

Water-soluble fabric-marking pen

OPTIONAL: Embroidery needle and embroidery floss for blanket-stitching around appliqués

SCRAPPY TABLECLOTH

This appliquéd tablecloth makes a cheerful centerpiece for a brunch table and is a great way to use scraps of fabric with large, interesting motifs. You can start with a vintage tablecloth, or follow the instructions here to make your own tablecloth using 44"- or 60"-wide linen (available in most home-decorating stores and many fabric shops).

Preparation

If you are making a new tablecloth, prepare your fabric by washing and drying it; then iron it thoroughly. Following the instructions on page 148, true and block the fabric. If you are starting with a vintage tablecloth, skip to Step 5.

Sewing Instructions

1 Fold Tablecloth's Edges
With the fabric wrong side up, fold and press each edge ¼" to the wrong side, but do not sew the pressed edges.

2 Miter Corners
Start on one corner and measure 2" from its point in each direction, as shown in the drawing on page 30. Mark these points with a small dot using your water-soluble marking pen. Using a straightedge and the water-soluble pen, connect the dots with a diagonal line. Fold and press the corner down along this line, as shown. Repeat this process at each corner. Using your iron, fold and press each edge again by 1" to the wrong side, creating mitered corners.

3 Edge-Stitch Folded Edges
Pin each pressed edge in several places, and edge-stitch (see page 155) the fold's inner edge, starting at one corner and lockstitching (see page 153) the beginning and end of the seam, as described in Step 3 of the napkin directions on page 27. Then when you get to the next corner, stop, with your needle down; lift the presser foot; and pivot the fabric into position to sew the next side. Once you've positioned the fabric, lower the presser foot, and continue sewing as above until you reach the point where you began edge-stitching, and lockstitch the end of the seam. Then clip the thread tails close to the fabric.

② Miter Corners

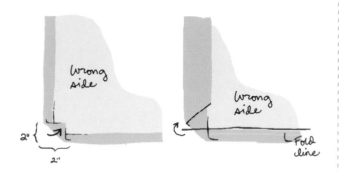

3-4 Edge-stitch Folded Edges and Hand-Sew Miter Closed

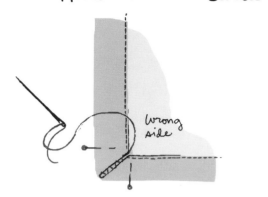

④ Hand-Sew Miter Closed

Using a hand-sewing needle, slipstitch (see page 155) each corner's miter closed.

⑤ Cut Out Appliqués

Lay the double-sided fusible interfacing on your ironing board with the interfacing's protective backing side down and the resin side up. Place one of your fat quarters or your printed fabric, right side up, over the interfacing, and press as directed by the interfacing's instructions to fuse the interfacing to the fabric. Use the water-soluble marking pen to draw a line around the image or area in the fat quarter or printed fabric that you want to use as an appliqué, and cut out the appliqué.

⑥ Attach Appliqués

Peel the protective backing off the interfaced appliqué, and position the appliqué on your tablecloth. Set your iron according to the interfacing's instructions for your tablecloth fabric, and press the appliqué to fuse it to the fabric.

If you want to add a decorative touch and further secure the edges of your appliqué, thread your embroidery needle with embroidery floss, and hand-stitch around the appliqué's edge with a blanket stitch (see page 47), tying off the floss on the fabric's wrong side.

⑤ Cut Out Appliqués

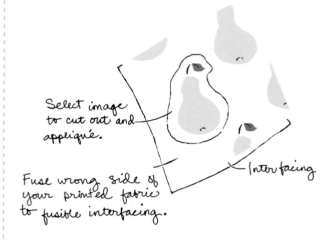

Select image to cut out and appliqué.

Fuse wrong side of your printed fabric to fusible interfacing.

Interfacing

This soup is a perfect, simple supper for fall or winter paired with a glass of dry white wine and a salad. I roast the squash early in the day, so my house smells wonderful while I sew and listen to music. I find that neighbors and friends who come by end up staying for supper. Once I even snared the UPS man.

SQUASH SOUP

Makes approximately 4 servings, 1½ cups each.

3 small acorn squash (2-3 lbs total)

1 small butternut squash (2-3 lbs)

2 cloves garlic, peeled

2 large shallots

5 tablespoons extra-virgin olive oil

½ cup whipping cream

4 to 6 cups vegetable stock

1 tablespoon Kosher salt, plus more to taste

White or cayenne pepper, to taste

Preheat oven to 400 degrees F. Cut squash into halves, and spoon out seeds. Place squash on baking sheets. Chop shallots and garlic, and mix with olive oil and 1 tablespoon kosher salt. Spoon shallots/garlic mixture into squash cavities. Bake for about 1 hour 15 minutes, or until squash is soft.

Remove squash from oven. Scoop out squash's soft flesh, garlic, and shallots, and put into large pot. Add 4 cups vegetable stock, and simmer. While mixture is heating, use hand-held food processor (or blender) to blend soup as it heats. Add additional vegetable stock to get desired consistency—it should slide easily off wooden spoon, leaving creamy coating. Heat mixture until it almost boils; then reduce to low heat, and simmer 20 minutes. Remove soup from heat, and add whipping cream, and kosher salt and white pepper to taste.

Finished Dimensions

Small bag: 7" x 6"

Medium bag: 12" x 11"

Large bag: 19½" x 17"

Materials

NOTE: *Choose sheeting, poplin, or quilting cotton for small and medium bags, and heavy linen, denim, or canvas for large bag.*

45"-wide woven fabric:

   Small bag: 14" x 9", cut into 2 rectangles, 7" x 9"

   Medium bag: ½ yard, cut into 2 rectangles, 12" x 15"

   Large bag: ¾ yard, cut into 2 rectangles, 18" x 23"

¼"-wide *(or narrower) drawstring (like string, twill tape, ribbon, or spaghetti strap [see page 156]):* for small bag, 1 yard; medium bag, 1½ yards; large bag, 2½ yards

All-purpose thread to match fabric

Seam ripper

Straightedge ruler

Water-soluble fabric-marking pen

Choosing Fabric

I used a plain muslin fabric for the largest bag and quilting cottons for the smaller ones. This pattern will work with almost any weight of woven fabric.

DRAWSTRING TRAVEL BAGS

These bags are perfect for holding shoes and small items when en route. The largest size is ideal for boots or laundry, and the smallest size will hold all the tiny things that tend to disappear into the deepest corners of a suitcase. I "boxed" the corners of the largest bag to create a flat bottom. I made spaghetti straps for the drawstring, but you can substitute anything from ribbon to twill tape to twine.

Preparation

Wash, dry, and "true" the fabric (see page 148) before cutting it to give your bag a straight, neat appearance and to make sewing much easier.

Sewing Instructions

NOTE: *Instructions are given for the large bag, with directions for the medium and small bags in parentheses.*

❶ Sew Bag's Side and Bottom Edges

Pin the two rectangles together, with right sides facing and the edges aligned. Designate the top of the bag as the short end that orients any print or design on the fabric so that it runs in the correct direction. Then join the rectangles' two side and bottom edges with a ⅜" seam, backstitching (see page 153) at the beginning and end of the seam and removing the pins as you sew.

❷ "Box" Bag's Bottom Corners (optional for smaller bags)

With the bag still turned wrong side out, press open the seam along the side and bottom edges. Then iron the corner flat, as shown in the drawing on page 34. Measure 2" (1", ½") from the point of one corner on each side, and mark those two points with a dot using a water-soluble disappearing-ink pen. Connect the dots with a straightedge ruler and the water-soluble pen, and pin and sew along the marked lines. When you turn the bag right side out in the next step, the corners will be "boxed" and the bottom flat.

❷ "Box" Bag's Bottom Corners

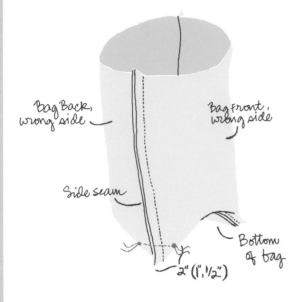

Bag Back, wrong side

Bag Front, wrong side

Side seam

Bottom of bag

2" (1", ½")

4-5 Create Drawstring Opening in Casing, Then Insert and Tie Drawstrings

Zigzag-stitch to reinforce points where casing seams intersect side seam; then open side seam with seam ripper.

Attach safety pin to end of drawstring to guide it through casing.

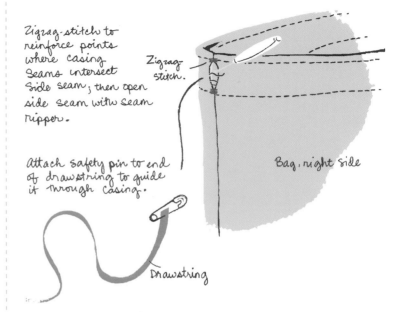

Zigzag stitch.

Bag, right side

Drawstring

❸ Sew Casing for Drawstring

Topstitch second row to create casing.

Edge-stitch folded edge

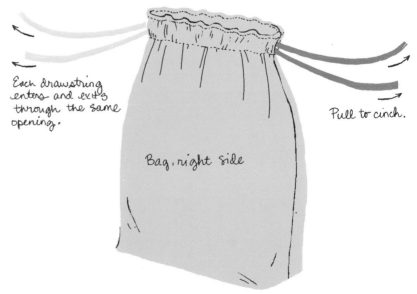

Each drawstring enters and exits through the same opening.

Bag, right side

Pull to cinch.

❸ Sew Casing for Drawstring

With the bag still wrong side out, fold down its top edge ¼" to the wrong side, and press the fold. Fold this edge again to the wrong side, this time 2" (1", ¾"), and press the double fold. Edge-stitch (see page 155) the upper edge of the double fold.

Turn the bag right side out, and press the side seams flat. Sew a second row of stitches 1½" (½", ¼") from the top edge of the bag to create a casing for the drawstring.

❹ Create Drawstring Opening in Casing

Set your machine for a zigzag stitch with a very short length and medium width, and stitch back and forth generously for ⅛" at the two points where the casing's horizontal seams intersect one side seam. Then use a seam ripper to cut through the side-seam stitches in the top fabric layer *only* between the casing seams to create an opening for the drawstring. Repeat the process on the other side seam.

❺ Insert and Tie Drawstrings

Cut the drawstring in half. Attach a safety pin to one end of one drawstring, and thread the drawstring through the entire casing, pulling it out through the same opening into which you inserted it. Remove the safety pin, and tie the drawstring's two ends together with a secure knot.

Repeat the process with the second drawstring, inserting this drawstring through the opening on the opposite side seam. You should now be able to pull both loops and cinch the bag tightly closed.

RIGHT A drawstring bag is also a perfect way to wrap a gift—especially a handmade one.

Finished Dimensions

16" x 34 ½"

Materials

½ yard of 36"-wide linen or cotton toweling (*makes two towels*)

Scrap, at least 3" x 1½", of contrasting or coordinating, lightweight woven fabric for loop

All-purpose thread to match fabric

Elastic thread

1 button (*I used a ⅝" button*)

Hand-sewing needle

Loop turner (*see page 152*)

Choosing Fabric

I especially like Irish linen for this project because it becomes more absorbent with age and its smooth surface is good for buffing and drying glasses. You could also use toweling, which has a loose twill weave and soaks up lots of water; or you could choose real terrycloth, which is like a lightweight version of bath toweling.

GOOD-GUESTS-DO-THE-DISHES DISH TOWEL

This nifty little all-purpose dish towel lives happily on my refrigerator-door handle, with its loop and button securing it in place, poised to wipe a dish or to be wrapped around a waist when needed.

Sewing Instructions

❶ Cut Fabric

"True" the fabric (see page 148) to get it ready for cutting and sewing. For each towel, cut a 35" x 17" rectangle from your main fabric and a strip 3" x 1½" from your scrap fabric.

❷ Make Stretchy Loop

Make a stretchy loop for hanging the towel by, first, folding the 3" x 1½" scrap strip lengthwise, with right sides together. Using elasticized thread wound in your bobbin (see page 155), sew the rectangle's long edges together with a ¼" seam, leaving long thread tails at the beginning and end of your seam.

Use the loop turner to turn the loop right side out (see page 152), and then press it flat. Tie and knot the two ends of the elasticized thread tails together to make a loop.

❸ Sew Towel's Edge and Finish

Turn each edge of the cut towel ⅛" to the wrong side and press the fold; then repeat the process to make double-folded edges. Tuck the joined edges of the loop under the towel's folded edge near the top right corner. Then set your machine to a short stitch length (see page 153), and edge-stitch (see page 155) continuously around all the double-folded edges, catching the loop's edges as you sew. Hand-sew your button (see page 157) on the corner of the short edge opposite the loop. Press the towel flat.

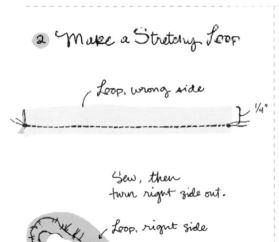

② Make a Stretchy Loop

Loop, wrong side

¼"

Sew, then turn right side out.

Loop, right side

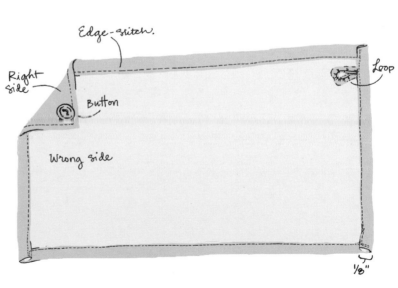

③ Sew Towel's Edges and Finish Towel.

Edge-stitch.

Right side

Button

Wrong side

Loop

⅛"

GROUND CLOTH/PUP TENT AND PILLOW

An old Girl Scout guide declares that "every girl should know how to make a safe and warm shelter from her blanket, should the need arise." Or maybe if the need arises for a nap or a bit of shade in your own backyard!

Fortunately, making a sturdy, washable ground cloth out of a heavy twill is easy, requiring only straight stitches. Adding loops at each corner and on each side enables you to anchor the edges on windy days or make yourself or your kids a little tent. I stuck knitting needles into the ground to hold down my corners, but tent stakes will also work. A pillow, in complementary fabric, makes your new spot comfy.

Sewing Ground Cloth / Pup Tent

❶ Cut and Sew Fabric Rectangles
Cut the fabric as shown in the Cutting Diagram on page 40. Then, with right sides together and the edges aligned, sew B and C together along one short edge with a 1" seam. Align sections A and B/C, with right sides facing, and sew them together along one long edge with a 1" seam.

❷ Press Edges, Insert Loops, and Topstitch
Fold and press each edge of the new rectangle ¼" to the wrong side, and then fold and press each edge again 1" to the wrong side. Insert and pin in place one of the six twill or bias-tape sections folded in half to form a loop beneath the pressed, folded edge at each corner and in the center of the rectangle's two short sides.

Topstitch along the folded, pressed edges on all four sides, catching the loops in the seam and removing the pins as you sew. To reinforce the loops at each corner, stitch up to the intersecting folded edge at the corner, pivot the fabric 90 degrees to stitch out to the fabric's edge, then pivot the fabric 180 degrees to stitch back over the loop, and continue topstitching the edge on this side (see the detail drawing on page 40).

Finished Dimensions

Ground Cloth/Pup Tent, 68" x 64"
Pillow, 16" square

Materials

For Ground Cloth/Pup Tent

3 yards of 60"-wide, washable, home-décor-weight fabric (like twill, canvas, or denim)

All-purpose thread to match fabric

1 yard of twill tape or 1 ½"-wide double-folded bias tape, sewn together along edges and cut into six 3" sections

15-20' of sturdy rope, cut into two lengths, for tent

6 knitting needles, 4 for tent

For Pillow

½ yard mid- to heavyweight, 44"- or 60"-wide fabric (optional for contrasting pillow, or use blanket-fabric remnant)

All-purpose thread to match fabric

Point turner

16"-square pillow form

Choosing Fabric

Choose a denim or twill that will soften with age and that has plenty of body. A print, like the one pictured, will cast interesting shadows inside and look lovely in your garden or yard.

Sewing and Installing Pup Tent

1 Cut and Sew Fabric Rectangles

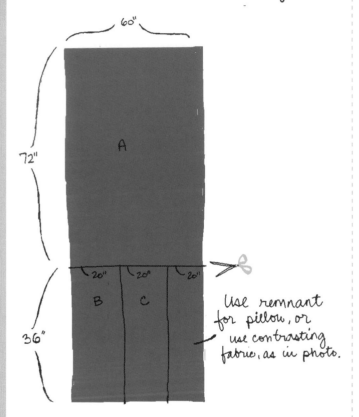

60"

72"

A

36"

20"   20"   20"

B   C

Use remnant for pillow, or use contrasting fabric, as in photo.

2 Press Edges, Insert Loops, and Topstitch

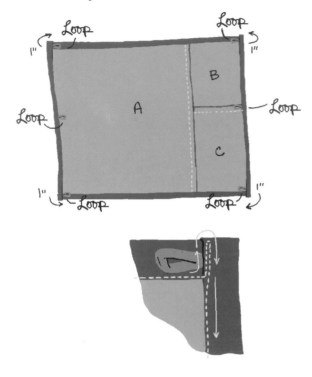

Loop   Loop

1"   1"

Loop   A   B   Loop

C

1"   1"

Loop   Loop

3-4 Tie Ropes Through Loops and Around Trees, and Stake Corners With Knitting Needles

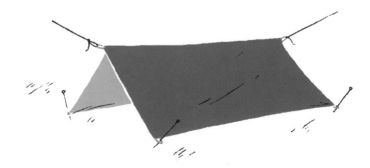

❸ Tie Ropes Through Loops and Around Trees

To set up your tent, find a spot in your yard with two trees 15' or less apart to use as anchors. Tie a length of rope through the center loop on one short end of the tent and then around the tree, hoisting the tent about 3½' off the ground. Repeat on the tent's other side, making the top of the tent straight and parallel with the ground.

❹ Stake Corners with Knitting Needles

Pull each corner out, and secure it in place using a knitting needle pushed through the loop and into the ground.

Sewing Pillow

❶ Cut Fabric and Finish Edges

Start by cutting the fabric remnant left from making the ground cloth/pup tent (or your ½ yard of contrasting fabric), so it measures 36" x 17". Turn and press each short end of the fabric ¼" to the wrong side, and then turn and press this edge ½" to the wrong side. Edge-stitch (see page 155) the top edge of the double fold, backstitching (see page 153) at the beginning and end of the seam.

❷ Fold Fabric and Sew

Fold the fabric into thirds with right sides facing and the short edges overlapping, so the width of the folded fabric equals 16". Make sure the top and bottom edges are aligned, and then pin and sew these two edges. Clip the corners.

❸ Turn Pillow Right Side Out and Shape Corners

Turn the pillow right side out, using a point turner to push the corners into shape. Insert a 16" pillow form into the opening in the back.

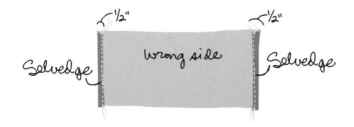

Sewing Pillow

❶ Cut Fabric and Finish Edges

½"   ½"

Selvedge   wrong side   Selvedge

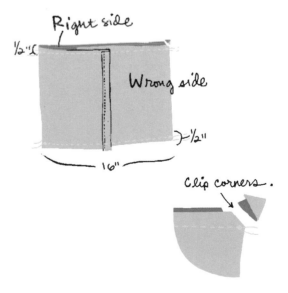

❷ Fold Fabric and Sew

Right side

½"   Wrong side

½"

16"

Clip corners.

Finished Dimensions

28 ¼" wide x 20" long

Materials

1 ⅛ yards of woven fabric
(for pillowcase)

44" of 2"-wide fabric
(for contrasting or
complimentary trim)

All-purpose thread to match fabric

Choosing Fabric

These pillowcases can be made
from a variety of woven fabrics. I
like to use brushed, or "sanded,"
poplins, but flannels and shirting
fabrics will work well too.

Preparation

Wash and dry the pillowcase and
trim fabrics. Lay the fabrics flat,
and "true" them (see page 148).
Being careful to cut with the grain
line (see page 149), cut a rectangle
33 ⅝" x 41" from the pillowcase
fabric and a rectangle 2" x 44"
from the trim fabric.

GUEST-ROOM PILLOWCASE

Homemade pillowcases, which can be sewn from a variety of
woven fabrics, add a unique touch to any sleep-over. Adding
a monogram or appliqué can be a great way to personalize
this project, but be sure to make these embellishments only
along the hem, leaving the main body of the pillowcase soft
and supple.

Sewing Instructions

❶ Prepare and Position Trim Strip

Prepare the trim strip by folding the fabric in half lengthwise, with wrong sides together, and pressing it. Lay the cut pillowcase fabric flat and right side up. Place the folded trim strip on top of the pillowcase fabric so that the trim's raw edges are 11" from the pillowcase fabric's right edge.

❷ Attach Trim Strip

Fold the right edge of the pillowcase fabric over the trim strip, and pin through all layers along this edge to keep the trim in place. Sew this edge with a ³/₈" seam. Open up the pillowcase fabric, revealing the trim, and press the fabric and trim flat.

❸ Sew Pillowcase's Edges

Bring up the bottom edge of the rectangle to fold the pillowcase in half, with right sides together. Stitch all the way around the folded rectangle's left and top edges, backstitching (see page 153) at the beginning and end of the ³/₈" seam. Trim off the excess trim fabric, and clip the pillowcase's corners.

❹ Finish Top Edge

Fold over the rectangle's raw right edge ¼" to the wrong side, and press the edge. Then fold this edge again until the trim strip just shows, and press and pin the edge in place. Edge-stitch (see page 155) the lower folded edge to the pillowcase. Turn the pillowcase right side out and press it.

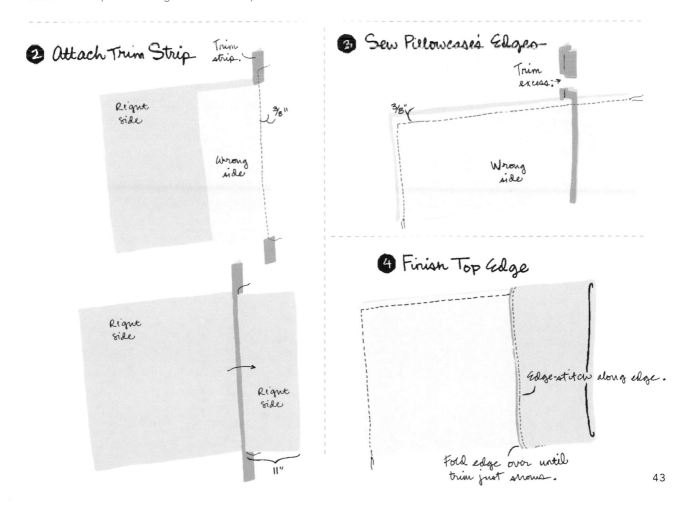

❷ Attach Trim Strip

Trim strip.

Right side

³/₈"

Wrong side

Right side

Right side

11"

❸ Sew Pillowcase's Edges

Trim excess.

³/₈"

Wrong side

❹ Finish Top Edge

Edge-stitch along edge.

Fold edge over until trim just shows.

GUEST-ROOM SLIPPERS

Imagine how welcome your weekend guest will feel if her room is stocked with a special new pair of slippers. These are modeled after the classic pink ballet shoe.

Sewing Instructions

NOTE: *After cutting out pattern in Step 1, directions below refer to only one slipper. Repeat Steps 2-9 to make second slipper.*

1 Lay Out and Cut Pattern

Trace (see page 149) the multi-size pattern, following the lines for your desired size, and cut out the traced pattern. Lay out the pattern pieces as shown in the Layout Diagram on page 46, and cut 2 Outer Slippers, 2 Slipper Linings, 2 Footbed Linings, and 2 Soles. Use a water-soluble pen to label each cut piece, and transfer the dots on the front toe from the pattern pieces to the cut fabric pieces.

2 Make Heel Loop

Edge-stitch (see page 155) closed one length of double-folded bias tape. Then fold the tape into a loop, and edge-stitch across its short edges.

3 Sew Heel Seam

Fold and pin one Outer Slipper in half with the right sides together and the edges aligned. Sew the heel with a ⅜" seam, and press the seam open (see page 155). Repeat the process for the Slipper Lining.

4 Layer and Sew Slipper Pieces and Rickrack

Layer the slipper pieces as follows: Slipper Lining, right side up; loop pinned at the lining's heel seam, facing down; one length of rickrack pinned at edge of lining's inner opening, with its ends overlapping by about 1" at the heel seam; and the Outer Slipper wrong side up. Note that the rickrack trim should be positioned so that about ⅛" shows above the top edge of the layered pieces.

Stitch all the way around the slipper's inside edge, removing the pins as you sew. Clip the excess rickrack ends to about ¼" each (the remaining ends will be hidden inside the slipper when it's turned right side out in Step 5).

5 Sew Elastic at Heel

With the slipper still turned wrong side out, pin the elastic in place, positioning one of its ends 2¼" from one side of the heel seam and stretching the elastic as you pin it from this point to 2¼" on the other side of the heel seam.

① Lay Out and Cut Pattern

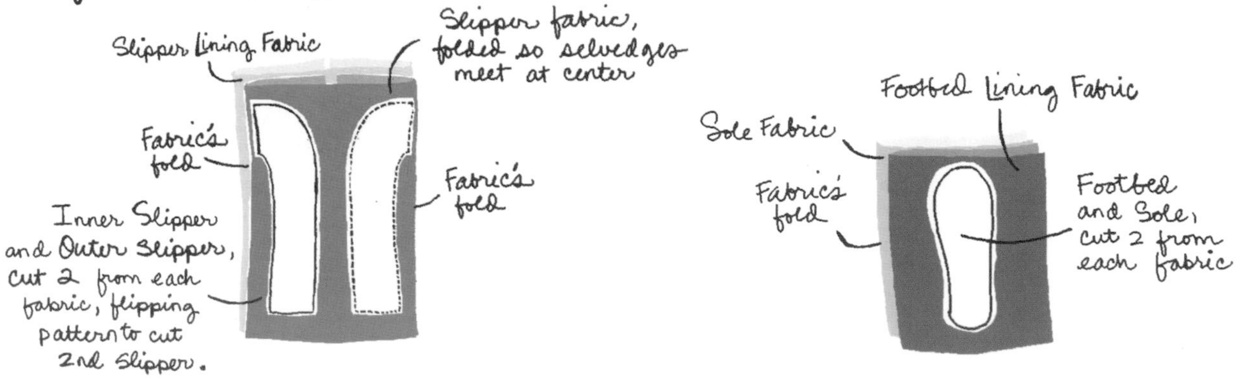

Slipper Lining Fabric

Slipper fabric, folded so selvedges meet at center

Fabric's fold

Inner Slipper and Outer Slipper, cut 2 from each fabric, flipping pattern to cut 2nd Slipper.

Fabric's fold

Sole Fabric

Footbed Lining Fabric

Fabric's fold

Footbed and Sole, cut 2 from each fabric

② Make Heel Loop

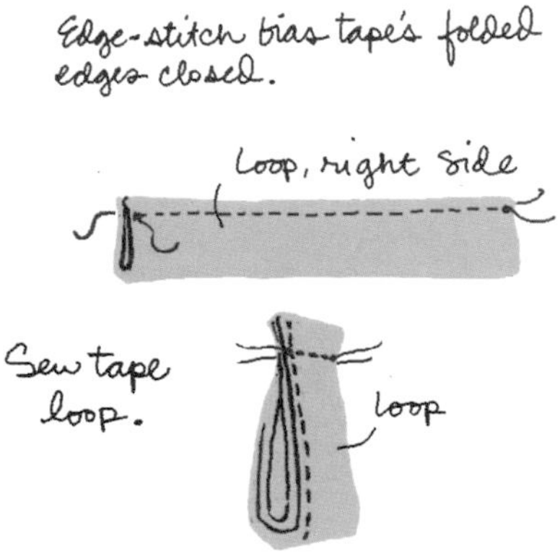

Edge-stitch bias tape's folded edges closed.

Loop, right side

Sew tape loop.

loop

③ Sew Heel Seam

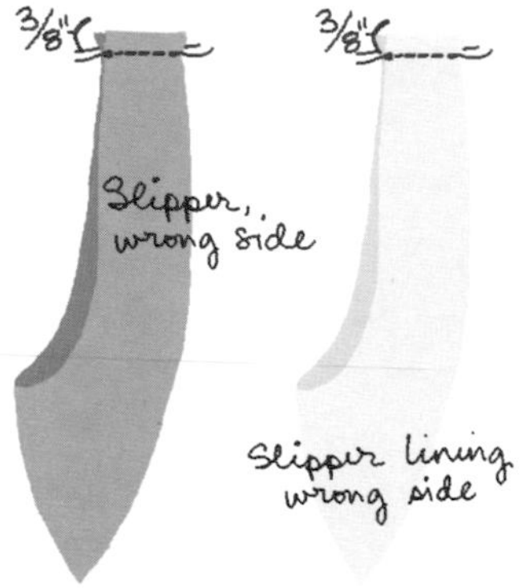

3/8"   3/8"

Slipper, wrong side

Slipper lining wrong side

④ Layer and Sew Slipper Pieces and Rickrack

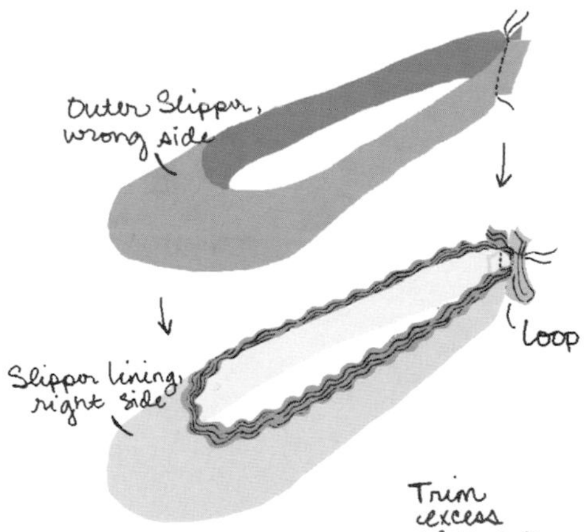

Outer Slipper, wrong side

Slipper lining, right side

Loop

Trim excess rickrack.

Slipper lining, wrong side

Slipper, wrong side

⑤ Sew Elastic at Heel

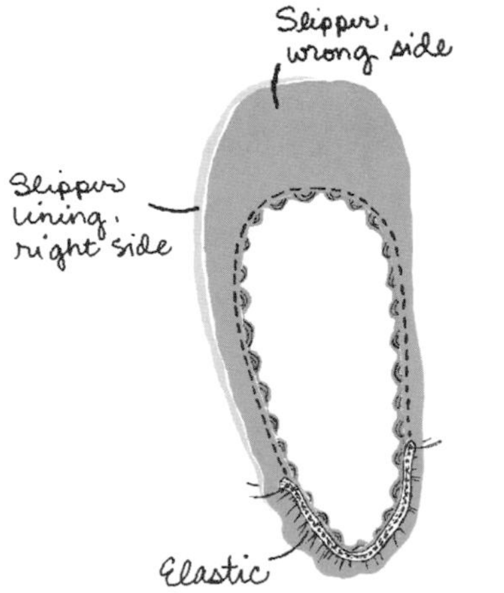

Slipper, wrong side

Slipper lining, right side

Elastic

⑥-⑦ Sew Outer Edge and Gather Slipper's Front Edge

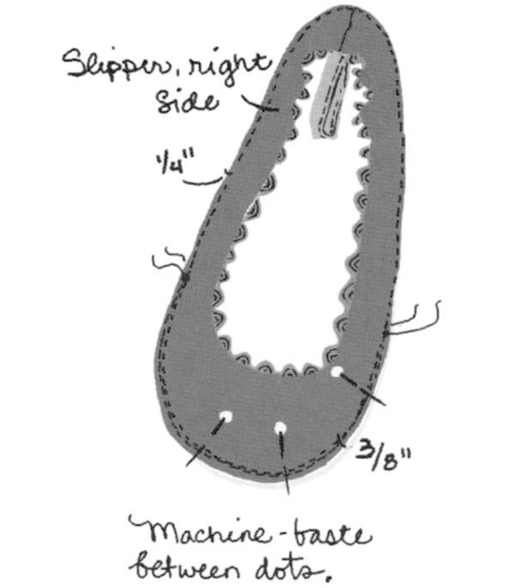

Slipper, right side

1/4"

3/8"

Machine-baste between dots.

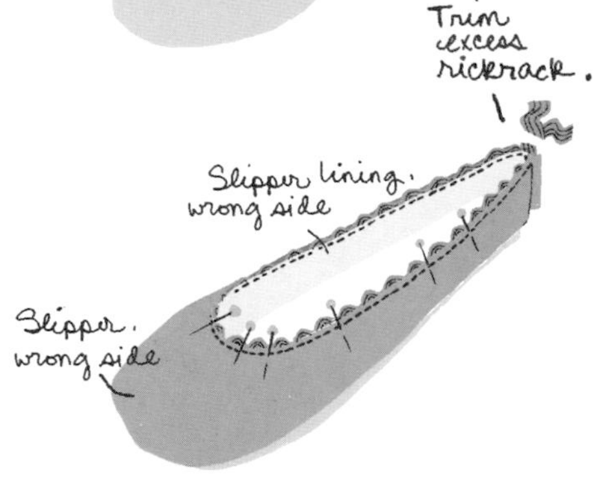

46

Set your machine for a medium-length and -width zigzag stitch, and stitch the elastic to the slipper, sewing along the previous stitching line that joins the Outer Slipper and lining, stretching the elastic and removing the pins as you sew. Use pinking shears to carefully trim around the inside edge of the seam, cutting away the excess rickrack trim and loop ends at the heel. Turn the slipper right side out and press it.

⑥ Sew Outer Edge of Slipper and Lining
With the slipper turned right side out, match and pin the bottom edges of the Outer Slipper and Slipper Lining, with wrong sides together. Stitch the edges together with a ¼" seam, removing the pins as you sew.

❼ Gather Slipper's Front Edge
Machine-baste (see page 153) the front edge of the slipper between the transferred dots, stitching ⅜" from the edge and leaving thread tails at both ends of the stitching. Pull the thread tails to create gathers around the slipper's toe. Press the slipper flat.

⑧ Sew Slipper to Insole
Starting at the heel and working towards the dots, pin the slipper to the insole, with the right sides of the footbed and Slipper Lining facing together. Adjust and pin the gathers around the front of the slipper, so the edges match up evenly. Stitch the footbed to the slipper, using a ¼" seam and removing the pins as you sew. Trim the seam allowance with pinking shears.

❹ Sew Slipper to Sole
Put your hand inside the front of the slipper, and shape the toe area, stretching out the gathers and encouraging the front of the slipper to take shape. With the bottom of the slipper facing you, use your iron to press the pinked edges towards the center of the inside. Use pinking shears to trim the edge of the felted wool sole. Then use a hand-sewing needle; the buttonhole, carpet, and craft thread; and a blanket-stitch (see the drawing below) to attach the felted wool sole to the slipper.

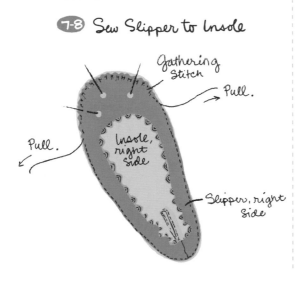

7-8 Sew Slipper to Insole

Gathering Stitch

Pull.

Pull.

Insole, right side

Slipper, right side

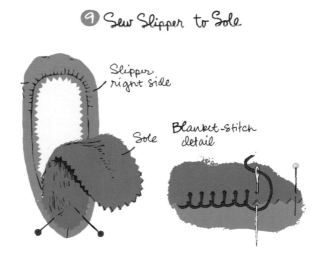

9 Sew Slipper to Sole

Slipper right side

Sole

Blanket-stitch detail

Finished Dimensions

6" x 9" x 4 ½"

Materials

⅛ yard or one fat quarter (*see page 26*) bottom-weight fabric (*see below; for outside of bag*)

⅛ yard or one fat quarter of lining fabric (*for lining*)

16" plastic zipper (*a thick jacket zipper works best; a metal zipper will rust if it gets wet*)

Zipper foot for your sewing machine

Hand-sewing needle

Safety pins

All-purpose thread to match both fabrics

Elastic thread, wound loosely around a bobbin

Water-soluble fabric-marking pen

Pinking shears

Weekend-Away Travel Bag pattern (*see pullout pattern sheet at back of book*)

Choosing Fabric

Choose a bottom-weight fabric with lots of body, like a twill or canvas, for the outside of this bag. Many home décor upholstery fabrics are treated with a water-resistant, stain-resistant finish and will work well. I chose a busy print for the lining for its stain-hiding powers—and because I love seeing it peeking out around my toiletries.

WEEKEND-AWAY TRAVEL BAG

This bag looks cute enough to reside permanently on the edge of the bathroom sink and is roomy enough to hold just about everything you need for a trip.

Sewing Instructions

① Lay Out and Cut Pattern

Wash and press the fabrics, and fold them in half across their width so that any print or nap direction on the fabric runs vertically on the bag (see the drawing on page 50). Trace (see page 149) the pattern, and cut it out. Then lay out the pattern, as shown, and cut 2 Top Panels, 2 Top Panel Linings, 1 Bag Body, 1 Bag Body Lining, 2 Side Panels, 2 Side Panel Linings, and 1 optional Pocket. Use the water-soluble marking pen to transfer to the cut pieces the pattern marks for the opening on the Bag Body.

② Prepare Top Panels

Fold and press the curved edge of the two Top Panels ¼" to the wrong side. Repeat with the two Top Panel Lining pieces.

③ Sew Top Panels to Zipper

Replace the regular stitching foot on your machine with the zipper foot, and set the stitch length to medium. Then sandwich the zipper between the long, straight edges of one Top Panel and one Top Panel Lining, with the fabrics' right sides together and the bottom edges of the panel, panel lining, and zipper aligned (the zipper teeth will be hidden between the panel and lining). Pin the sandwiched zipper tape in place, positioning the pins perpendicular to the tape, and stitch alongside the zipper teeth, as shown, removing the pins as you sew. Repeat the process to attach the other Top Panel and Top Panel Lining to the other side of the zipper.

④ Topstitch Around Zipper

Press the top panel (now your zipper panel) flat, lining up the folded, curved edges as evenly as possible (be careful when pressing around the zipper since a very hot iron can easily melt plastic). With your zipper foot still attached, topstitch the zipper panel as shown, about ⅛" from where your fabric meets your zipper, on both sides. Replace zipper foot with regular presser foot.

⑤ Edge-Stitch Zipper Panel

Align and pin the folded, unsewn, curved edges of the zipper panel and zipper panel lining, and edge-stitch (see page 155) them together.

1 Lay Out and Cut Pattern

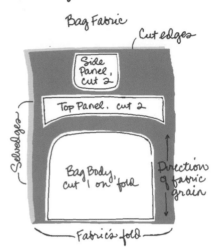

Bag Fabric

Cut edges

Side Panel, cut 2

Top Panel, cut 2

Selvedges

Bag Body, cut 1 on fold

Direction of fabric grain

Fabric's fold

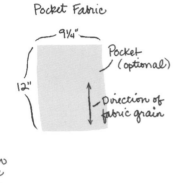

Lining Fabric

Cut edges

Side Panel Lining, cut 2

Top Panel Lining, cut 2

Bag Body Lining, cut 1 on fold

Direction of fabric grain

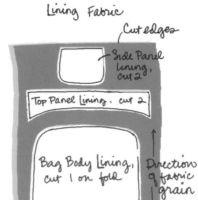

Pocket Fabric

9¼"

12"

Pocket (optional)

Direction of fabric grain

2-3 Prepare Top Panels and Sew to Zipper

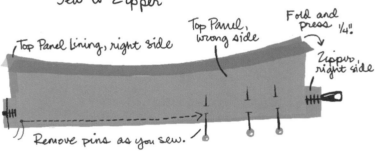

Top Panel Lining, right side

Top Panel, wrong side

Fold and press ¼"

Zipper, right side

Remove pins as you sew.

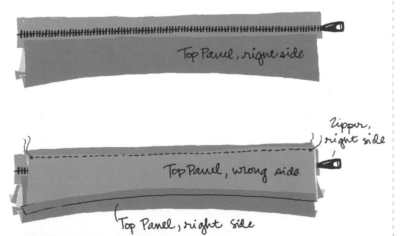

Top Panel, right side

Zipper, right side

Top Panel, wrong side

Top Panel, right side

4-5 Topstitch around Zipper, and Edge-stitch Curved Edges

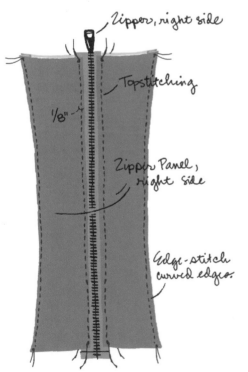

Zipper, right side

Topstitching

⅛"

Zipper Panel, right side

Edge-stitch curved edges.

🄖 Make Side Panels

To make the Side Panels, begin by folding over the top edge of one Side Panel ¼" to the wrong side, and press the fold, but don't sew it. Repeat this step with one Side Panel Lining. Place the Side Panel and lining with right sides facing, and sew the two pieces together with a ⅜" seam, backstitching (see page 153) at the beginning and end of the seam.

With pinking shears, trim the raw edges, turn the panel right side out, and press it. Repeat the process with the second Side Panel and lining.

🄗 Attach Side Panels to Zipper

Slip each end of your finished zipper panel into one Side Panel, with the Side Panel Lining facing up, so the Side Panel's edge just covers the beginning and end of the zipper. Secure the Side Panels in place with two safety pins, but do not sew them yet.

🄘 Make Optional Lining Pockets

(If you don't want pockets, skip to Step 10). With the wrong side of the fabric facing up, fold and press the long top edge ⅛" to the wrong side; then fold and press this edge again ½" to the wrong side. Repeat the process at the long bottom edge of pocket lining.

Load the bobbin wound with elastic thread into your machine (see page 155), and sew along the lining pocket's top, folded edge ⅜" from the edge, finishing and "gathering" the edge. Repeat the process on the bottom, folded edge. Liberally steam the pocket with your iron, and press the gathers flat, spacing the gathers as evenly as possible. If you're having trouble getting straight or even gathers, try pinning the pocket's top edge to the ironing board and tugging on the bottom edge as you press.

🄙 Attach Pockets to Lining

Lay the Pocket on top of the Bag Body Lining, with both fabrics right side up, and sew down the center of the pocket, backstitching at the beginning and end of the seam. Make pocket sections by stitching several perpendicular lines across the center stitching line, as shown, backstitching at the beginning and end of each seam.

🄗 Attach Side Panels to zipper

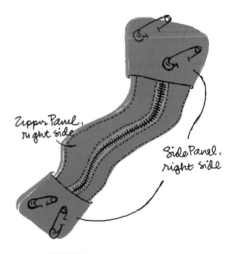

Zipper Panel, right side

Side Panel, right side

🄘 Make Optional Lining Pockets

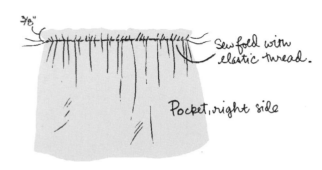

⅜"

Sew fold with elastic thread.

Pocket, right side

⑩ Join Bag Body and Lining

Align and sew the Bag Body and Bag Body Lining together, with right sides facing, leaving a 2-3" opening at the top, and backstitching at the dots transferred from the pattern. Turn the Bag Body right side out through the opening, and press the bag flat, turning under the seam allowances at the opening to match the rest of the seam.

⑪ Join Bag Body and Zipper Panel

Unzip the zipper, and pin the zipper panel into the Bag Body, as shown, with the right sides facing. If the edges do not match perfectly, remove the safety pins and adjust the amount of the zipper inside the side panels. Then sew all the way around the aligned edges with a ¼" seam, removing the pins as you sew and backstitching at the beginning and end of the seam. Turn the bag right side out through the zipper opening, and press the seams flat, using the pointed edge of your ironing board to shape the bag.

⑫ Slipstitch Side Panels

Using a doubled thread in a hand-sewing needle, slipstitch (see page 155) both Side Panels just below where the zipper teeth end, securing the zipper panel inside the Side Panels and finishing the edges. Try to sew small, even slipstitches; be sure to take a couple stitches at the beginning and end of the seam to secure it, and bury your beginning and ending knots in the lining. Remove the safety pins.

❾ Attach Pockets to Lining

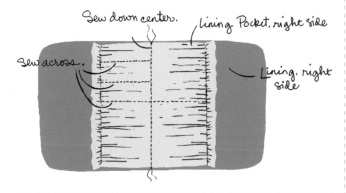

Sew down center.
Lining Pocket, right side
Sew across.
Lining, right side

❿ Join Bag Body and Lining

Bag Body Lining, right side
Bag Body, wrong side

⓫ Join Bag Body and Zipper Panel

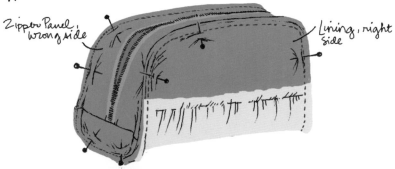

Zipper Panel, wrong side
Lining, right side

My Favorite Sewing Sounds

Chinatown, The Be Good Tanyas
When I saw the cover of this indie girl group's first CD, showing them in front of their makeshift camper-van tour bus wearing printed-cotton dresses, I wanted to quit my job and join them on tour, sewing curtains and floral frocks for their stage appearances; but the group never responded to my offer.

In Between Dreams, Jack Johnson
Singer/songwriter Johnson writes music when the weather is too stormy to surf. In this album, he found inspiration in lost love and banana pancakes.

Magic, Bruce Springsteen
Thirty-five years after I first saw Bruce Springsteen as a toddler sitting on my father's shoulders, Springsteen hit the road again with this collection to remind us all of exactly who we are and where we came from. I can't listen to this album without thinking of Mrs. G, my high-school home-economics teacher.

Songbird, Eva Cassidy
Eva Cassidy's tragically short career produced only a few albums, all worth adding to your collection. Each time I have sequestered myself in my studio to make a dress for an important occasion, I have chosen Songbird as my sound-track in hopes of channeling Cassidy's steady, perfect voice into my hands. It really seems to do the trick!

Music, Madonna
OK, I admit it. I could never have conjured up that two-piece silk-jersey number on page 90 without this album playing in the background. Like many of my generation, I grew up watching Madge's many reinventions of self, and have counted on her music more than once to help me emerge from a rut of same-old, same-old, a condition that afflicts every designer occasionally.

MORE FAVORITE STUDIO MUSIC

Chris Isaak (especially the album *Baja Sessions*)

Nancy Sinatra (who sewed many of her own fabulous stage outfits!)

Amy Winehouse

U2 (old and new)

Dusty Springfield

Feist (*The Reminder*, a great new classic)

Radiohead (especially *In Rainbows*)

QUICK GARDEN GLOVES

If you traced your hand to make a Thanksgiving turkey in the second grade, you are more than qualified to make these gloves. You will need a sewing machine with a zigzag stitch; a nice, sharp ball-point machine-sewing needle; and polyester or polyester-wrapped cotton thread. See page 153 for some helpful tips on sewing with a zigzag stitch.

Preparation

Fabric with spandex or Lycra can shrink a lot when washed, so it's important to wash, dry, and "true" (see page 148) the fabric *before* cutting and sewing. No matter how tempting it may be to try to speed up the process by skipping Step 1 and "tracing" your hand directly on the fabric, you will find that making a paper pattern will produce gloves that are exactly the same size.

Sewing Instructions

❶ Make Glove Pattern

Trace your hand on the sheet of paper, and then add a ⅛" seam allowance to the entire tracing. Use paper scissors to cut out the pattern piece.

❷ Trace and Cut Out Pattern

Fold your fabric right sides together twice, first horizontally, then vertically. Then lay the pattern on the fabric, as shown, and trace around the pattern with a water-soluble fabric-marking pen or, in the case of dark fabrics, with tailor's chalk.

Pin generously and carefully cut out your pattern pieces: two front gloves and two back gloves.

❸ Join Front and Back Gloves

Match up and pin each front and back glove with the right sides facing and the edges aligned.

To sew the front and back gloves together, you'll need to use a zigzag stitch since this stitch stretches, which is what's needed for a stretchy fabric like a knit. Set your sewing machine to a wide zigzag stitch with a short stitch-length, and start sewing at the outside wrist. Carefully stitch around each finger and back to the inside wrist. Repeat the process with the other glove.

❹ Finish Glove's Cuff

With the glove still turned wrong side out, turn the glove's unfinished cuff ¼" to the wrong side, and press the fold. Then zigzag-stitch this edge in place, capturing the raw edge underneath the zigzag stitches. Repeat the finishing process on the second glove, turn both gloves right side out using a point turner to shape fingers, and start gardening!

① Make Glove Pattern

add ⅛" to entire tracing.

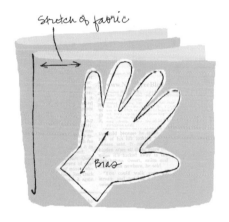

② Trace and Cut Out Pattern

Stretch of fabric

Bias

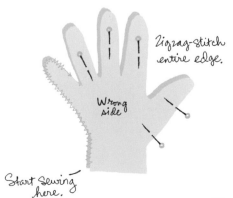

③ Join Front and Back Gloves, and Finish Glove's Edges

Zigzag-stitch entire edge.

Wrong side

Start sewing here.

Chapter 2

DRESSING UP AND DOWN

ALL-WEEKEND SUNDRESS

This dress is perfect for the most casual outings: a trip to the farmer's market, a stroll to the river, or a quick run to the fabric shop. I like the long length, but you can always make it shorter. The dress will work without the spaghetti straps, but I suggest sewing them in and tucking them out of the way if you don't want to use them all the time. You never know when a bit of added support will come in handy.

Preparation

To make sewing easier, wind two bobbins before starting your project: one with elastic thread and the other with all-purpose sewing thread to match your fabric. Load the bobbin with all-purpose sewing thread in your machine first for steps 1-7. Then switch to the bobbin with elastic thread to join the bodice and skirt and smock the dress.

Sewing Instructions

❶ Cut Fabric

Trace (see page 149) the multi-size pattern, following the lines for your desired size, and cut out the traced pattern. Then lay out your fabric flat, and place the pattern pieces as shown in the Layout Diagram on page 61. Note that while the Bodice Front and Bodice Back are two different pattern pieces, the Upper Skirt is a single pattern piece that needs to be cut twice. For the Skirt Ruffle, make two rectangles that are 60" x 20" out of your remaining fabric. Since the fabric is laid flat, you'll need to move the pattern piece for the Upper Skirt, as indicated by the dashed-line pattern pieces on the Layout Diagram, to cut the second piece for each. You will cut 1 Front Bodice, 1 Back Bodice, 2 Upper Skirts, and 2 Skirt Ruffles. Use the water-soluble fabric-marking pen to label each cut piece.

❷ Sew Upper Skirt

Position the two Upper Skirt panels, with the right sides together and their raw edges aligned, and sew the panels together with a ³/₈" seam, backstitching (see page 153) at the beginning and end of each seam. Press the seams flat (see page 155).

Finished Dimensions

NOTE: *Dress's waist and top are sewn with elastic thread, ensuring a snug fit.*

Small: Fits up to 36" bust, 29" waist, 38" hip

Medium: Fits up to 39" bust, 33" waist, 40" hip

Large: Fits up to 42" bust, 38" waist, 44" hip

Materials

3 yards of 44/45"-wide fabric or 2 ½ yards of 58/60"-wide fabric

3 yards of spaghetti strapping *(optional; available in many fabric and craft stores, or see page 156 to make your own)*

All-purpose thread to match fabric

Elastic thread

Measuring tape

Water-soluble fabric-marking pen

Hand-sewing needle

All-Weekend Sundress pattern *(see pullout pattern sheet at back of book)*

Choosing Fabric

This dress works best in a lightweight knit fabric, especially for curvy body types, but it also looks great made up in lightweight woven fabric with a bit of drape, like a rayon/linen blend or a voile. Avoid heavier fabrics for this project, such as twills, heavy linen, and quilting cotton, especially if you want to wear it without straps.

❸ Sew Skirt Ruffle

Position the two Skirt Ruffles, with right sides together and the short edges aligned. Sew the ruffles' short edges with a ⅜" seam, backstitching at the beginning and end of each seam. Press the seams flat.

Machine-baste (see page 153) the top edge of the Skirt Ruffle to gather it, sewing ¼" from the fabric's edge.

❹ Join Upper Skirt and Ruffle

Place the gathered Skirt Ruffle into the Upper Skirt, with right sides together, matching the skirt's bottom edge and the ruffle's top edge and aligning and pinning the side seams of the two pieces. Adjust the gathers on the Skirt Ruffle so that the two tubes are the same circumference and the gathers are equally distributed around the Skirt Ruffle. Finish aligning and pinning the two edges to be joined, and sew them with a ⅜" seam. Note that placing the Skirt Ruffle's gathered edge facing up under the needle with the Upper Skirt's flat edge facing down will make it easier to sew the two pieces together.

❺ Join Front and Back Bodice

Align and pin the side seams of the Front Bodice and Back Bodice with right sides together. Sew the side seams with a ⅜" seam, and press the seams flat.

❻ Finish Bodice's Top Edge

With the bodice still turned wrong side out, finish its top raw edge by, first, turning the edge ⅛" to the wrong side and pressing it, then turning and pressing the folded edge again, this time ⅜", to the wrong side. Press the folded edge again; then turn the bodice right side out, and edge-stitch (see page 155) the double-folded edge.

❼ Hem Skirt

Find your hem length by using a measuring tape to measure along your side from your natural waist to your desired hem length. Turn your skirt wrong side out, and measure down from the top of one of the side seams, and mark your desired hem length measurement with a water-soluble pen. Then measure and mark the hem length on the other side seam.

Next measure and mark 1½" below each of the marks you just made to provide for the hem itself, and draw a continuous line between these two marks around your skirt, following the skirt's edge. Cut along this marked line.

With the skirt still turned wrong side out, finish the skirt's hem by, first, turning the edge ¼" to the wrong side and pressing it, then turning it again 1¼" to the wrong side and pressing it. Then turn the skirt right side out to edge-stitch the double-folded hem.

❽ Join Bodice and Skirt

Replace the bobbin in your machine with the bobbin wound with elastic thread. Position the bodice and skirt sections, with right sides together and the side seams of the two pieces aligned. Join the two sections with a ½" seam, and press the seam flat.

❶ Cut Fabric

Selvedges

Upper Skirt, cut 2 on fold (Cut 1 here; then move pattern below.)

Fabric's fold

Upper Skirt, cut 2 on fold (Cut 2nd piece here.)

Front Bodice, cut 1 on fold

Back Bodice, cut 1 on fold

Fabric's fold

❸ Sew Skirt Ruffle

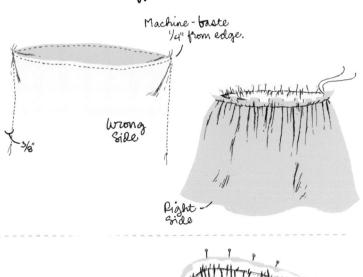

Machine-baste ¼" from edge.

Wrong Side

3/8"

Right Side

❹ Join Upper Skirt and Ruffle

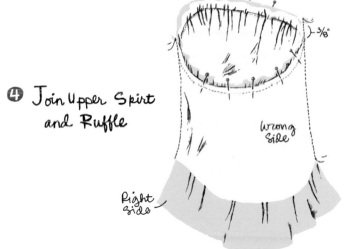

3/8"

Wrong Side

Right Side

❷ Sew Upper Skirt

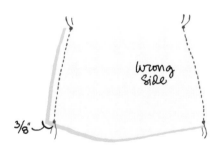

Wrong Side

3/8"

❺·❻ Join Front and Back Bodice and Finish Bodice's Top Edge

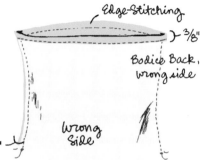

Edge-Stitching

3/8"

Bodice Back, wrong side

Wrong Side

3/8"

❼ Hem Skirt

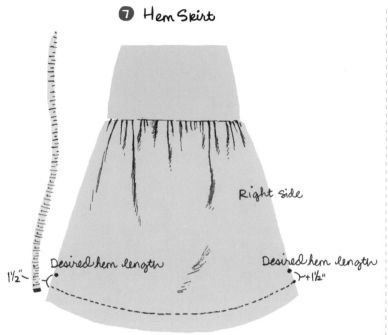

Right side

Desired hem length

Desired hem length +1½"

1½"

❽ Join Bodice and Skirt

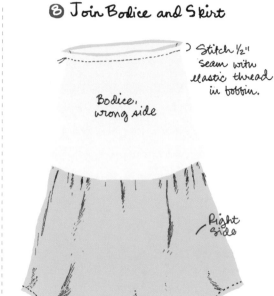

Stitch ½" seam with elastic thread in bobbin.

Bodice, wrong side

Right side

❾ Smock Bodice

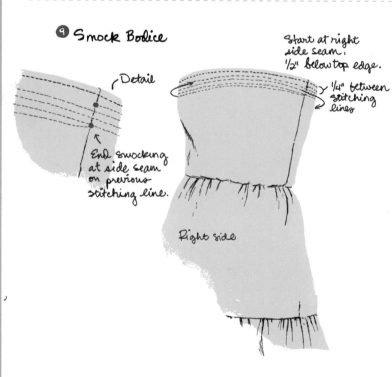

Detail

End smocking at side seam on previous stitching line.

Start at right side seam, ½" below top edge.

¼" between stitching lines

Right side

❿ Smock Waist

¼" between stitching lines

Start at right side seam, ½" below top edge.

Right side

❾ Smock Bodice

Before adding elastic smocking to the dress, read "Sewing With Elastic Thread" on page 155. To smock the bodice, start stitching at the right side seam ½" below the bodice's top edge. Sew parallel to the top edge until you reach the left side seam; then start slightly angling your stitches downward so that, when you reach the right side seam, your stitching line is ¼" below where you started. Continue sewing ¼" below and parallel to your previous stitching line, until you've sewn two and a half lines of smocking in what will be a tight spiral. On the last half-line (that is, on the back of the bodice), slightly angle your stitches upward, so that this stitching line ends where the previous stitching line crossed the right side seam.

❿ Smock Waist

Smock the waistline the same way you did in Step 9, beginning ½" below your waist seam. Make five rows of smocking for a size small or medium, or six rows for a size large or if you have a longer-than-average torso.

⑪ Add Optional Strap

If you want to add spaghetti straps, cut your purchased or made strap (see page 156) into two 20" lengths. Position each strap 4" from the side seam in front and 5 ½" from the side seam in back, and hand-sew the straps into position. Tie a knot in the end of each strap to keep it from fraying.

RIGHT Many jersey fabrics, including the one shown here, do not require hemming. If your fabric does not unravel easily, just cut its hem evenly and leave it "raw."

Finished Dimensions

Bag Body, 12" x 11½" x 1¾"

Materials

1 very supple piece of tanned leather, 5-6 square feet, no less than 22" x 34" *(leather is sold by the whole skin in large fabric stores and online)*

½ yard of lining fabric, cut into two 13" squares

Heavyweight thread to match leather

All-purpose thread to match lining and pocket

Sewing-machine needles: 1 universal and 1 for sewing leather

Zipper foot for sewing machine *(optional but recommended)*

5 D-rings, 1¼" wide *(available at craft stores)*

Lobster clasps: two, 2½" long *(should be narrow enough to fit through the D-rings); (available at craft stores)*

18" length of ¾"-wide double-sided fusible tape *(also called hem tape)*

Pressing cloth to protect leather *(linen dish towel or cotton scrap will work)*

Point turner

Choosing Fabric

If you don't want to use leather, this bag is also beautiful made up in a heavyweight canvas or cotton velveteen.

TOWN BAG

Grown-up and sophisticated in a buttery leather with a metallic finish, this bag will make you feel a little special on a Saturday morning, even if you're wearing it with a pair of jeans, sandals, and the shirt you slept in.

Don't be fearful of sewing on leather; almost any home-sewing machine can handle it. Just be sure to use a very supple piece of tanned leather, and a leather machine needle and heavyweight thread.

Sewing Instructions

❶ Cut Pattern Pieces

First, figure out how to best place the pattern pieces you'll need to cut from the leather: two 14" x 13" rectangles for the Bag Bodies, two 1" x 14" rectangles for the Side Panels, and one 1¼" x 34" rectangle for the Strap. If you can cut Strap as a single strip from your leather skin, do so. If not, cut the Strap in two or three sections, all 1¼" wide, whose combined length equals 34" plus a ⅜" seam allowance for each end of the pieces to be joined (for example, if you cut the strap in two pieces, you'll need to add four ⅜" seam allowances, or 1½", to the 34" length for a total length of 35½"). If you've cut the Strap in sections, sew them end to end, with their right sides together, with a ⅜" seam.

Before moving on to start sewing your bag, check your machine manual for instructions on sewing leather and how to adjust your machine, if possible, for sewing various thicknesses.

❷ Sew Side Seams of Lining and Bag

With the front and back Lining pieces right sides together and the edges aligned, sew the side seams with a ⅜" seam. Replace the universal needle in your machine with the leather needle and the all-purpose thread with the heavyweight thread, and repeat this step with your leather Bag Body pieces.

❸ Attach Side Panels

Attach Side Panels' top section: Because pins will leave permanent holes in leather, use fusible tape instead to position the Side Panels and hold them in place while sewing them to the purse. To do this, cut six lengths of ¾"-wide, double-sided fusible tape, two of them 1" long, two 3" long, and two 5" long. To fuse the hem tape to the Bag Body, begin by positioning one 1" strip of fusible tape over the top 1" of one of the bag's side seams. Then set your iron for medium heat; center the top 1" of one Side Panel over the fusible tape, with the top edges aligned; and cover the Side Panel with the pressing cloth. Press this section of the Side Panel to fuse it to the Bag Body.

Attach Side Panel's middle and bottom sections: Before attaching the Side Panel's middle section, slide the panel's free end through one of the D-rings, and make a half-loop in the panel by folding it. Then position the 3" length of fusible tape over the Bag Body's side seam, and repeat the process above to fuse the Side Panel's middle section to the Bag Body.

Slide the panel's free end through another D-ring, make a half-loop in the panel, position the 5" length of fusible tape over the bag's side seam, and repeat the process above to fuse the bottom section to the bag.

Finally, stitch across the Side Panel at each D-ring ¼" from the top of the folded edge holding the D-Ring, backstitching at the beginning and end of the seam.

❶ Cut Pattern Pieces

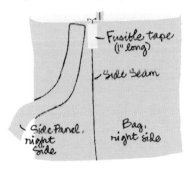

no less than 22" wide

14"
1¼"
14"
1"
Side Panel, cut 2
14"
13"
Bag Body, cut 2
No less than 34" long
Bag Body, cut 2nd piece here
Purse Strap cut 1 34" long
13"
Side Panel, cut 2nd piece here

❸ Attach Side Panels

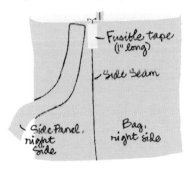

Fusible tape (1" long)
Side Seam
Side Panel, right side
Bag, right side

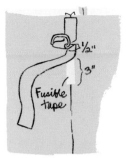

½"
3"
Fusible tape

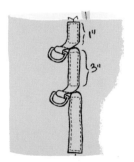

1"
3"

④ Sew Bottom Seam

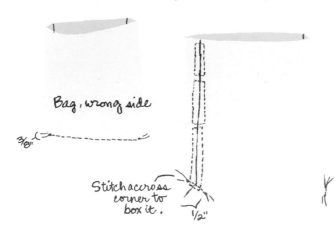

Bag, wrong side

3/8"

Stitch across corner to box it.

1/2"

⑤ Join Bag and Lining

1/4"

Lining, wrong side

Bag, right side

⑥ Sew Lining's Bottom Seam

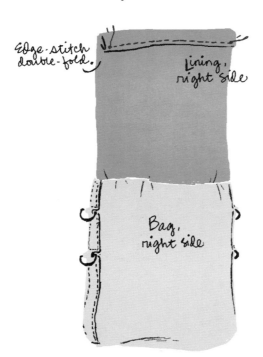

Edge-stitch double-fold.

Lining, right side

Bag, right side

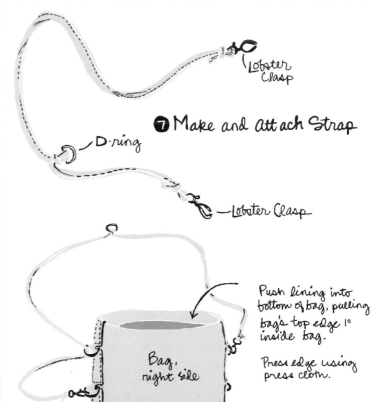

Lobster Clasp

D-ring

⑦ Make and Attach Strap

Lobster Clasp

Bag, right side

Push lining into bottom of bag, pulling bag's top edge 1" inside bag.

Press edge using press cloth.

Stitch Side Panel to Bag: Using the zipper foot on your machine, sew each section of the Side Panel to the purse ⅛" from the edge of the leather as follows: Sew the panel's top section, starting at the top of the Side Panel, sewing down one long side, and stopping, with the needle down, to pivot ⅜" above the half-loop holding the first D-ring. Sew across the panel at this point; stop again, with the needle down, to pivot ⅛" from the leather's edge; sew back up the panel's other long side; pivot at the top edge; and sew across the panel to your starting point.

(To secure the edge-stitching, be sure to begin sewing by setting the stitch length to zero and taking a couple of stitches in place before resetting the stitch length to its regular setting and continuing to sew. At the end of the edge-stitching, again set the stitch length to zero and take a couple stitches in place before removing the bag from under the needle. Finally, pull the top thread on the bag's right side to the lining side, knot it off with the bobbin thread, and stitch inside the lining to bury the thread tails.)

Starting ⅜" below the first D-ring, stitch the Side Panel's center section to the bag, as above (the distance between the stitching lines above and below the D-rings allows the D-rings to move freely). Then move to the Side Panel's bottom section, and stitch it in the same way to the bag.

❹ Sew Bottom Seam

Turn the Bag Body wrong side out, and sew the bottom edges together with a ⅜" seam. "Box" the corners, stitching across them diagonally, as shown in the drawing at left.

❺ Join Bag and Lining

Insert the Bag Body, right side out, inside the Lining tube, wrong side out, so that the right sides of the leather and lining fabric are facing together. Carefully sew along the top edge, ¼" from the edge.

❻ Sew Lining's Bottom Seam

Pull the Lining up out of the bag, and fold over together and press the Lining's bottom raw edges ⅛". Then fold and press these edges again ⅛", and edge-stitch (see page 155) the double-fold. Push the Lining back into the bottom of the bag, allowing it to pull the leather's top edge inside the bag by 1". With the pressing cloth covering the leather's top edge, press this edge with a warm, dry iron.

❼ Make and Attach Strap

Begin by folding the Strap leather in half, with wrong sides facing, and sewing the edges together with a ⅛" seam. Tie a D-ring on the Strap, about a third of the way from one end. Then tie a lobster clasp on each end of the Strap. Attach one lobster clasp to the lower D-ring on one Side Panel; thread the strap through the upper D-ring on that side, then through the upper D-ring and lower D-ring on the other Side Panel, and back up through the upper D-ring. Finally attach the clasp to the upper D-ring on the first side. (For a shorter Strap, use the lobster clasp on the Strap to adjust its length.)

Finished Dimensions

Width at top center, 7"; finished circumference, 22" *(adjustable)*

Materials

⅛ yard of lightweight woven fabric or fat quarter *(see page 26)* or scrap fabric measuring 10" x 18" *(quilting cotton works best, but lightweight linen also works well)*

All-purpose thread to match

5" of waistband elastic or 1"-wide elastic

JANE'S HEAD SCARF

The secret to this scarf is a strategically placed piece of elastic that holds it in place. This is a wonderful project for a lovely, but unused vintage scarf or a scrap of fabric that belongs in the limelight.

Sewing Instructions

① Cut Fabric

Cut out two rectangles, one measuring 17½" x 8" and one measuring 7½" x 3½".

② Finish Large Rectangle's Long Edges

On the large rectangle, turn and press the two long edges ⅛" to the wrong side twice. Then edge-stitch (see page 155) both double-folded edges.

③ Pleat Large Rectangle's Short Edges

Pleat and pin one short end of the large rectangle, so it measures 2". Edge-stitch across the pleats to secure them, and press the fabric. Repeat the process on the rectangle's other end.

④ Sew Pleated Ends to Elastic

Sew one of the pleated ends to one end of the elastic, using a medium-width zigzag stitch and wrapping the pleated end around the elastic's edge, as shown. It's a good idea at this point to "try on" your headband to see if it comfortably fits your head or is too loose, in which case you can cut the elastic to the appropriate length for you.

⑤ Finish Small Rectangle's Short Edges

On the small cut rectangle, turn each short edge ⅛" to the wrong side, press the fold, and edge-stitch it in place.

⑥ Make Small Rectangle into Tube

With the small rectangle's fabric right sides together, sew the rectangle's long edges together to form a small tube. Turn the tube right side out, and press it flat with the new seam centered on one side.

⑦ Join Headband and Tube

Push the end of the elastic through the tube until it comes out the other side. Position the tube over the elastic and the headscarf's first pleated edge, and topstitch the tube in place on this end. Adjust the tube to cover the elastic's second raw edge and headband's pleated ends, and topstitch this end of the tube in place. Press the finished headband.

③ Pleat Short Edges

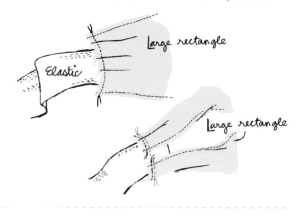

Large rectangle

Right side

2"

④ Sew Pleated Ends to Elastic

Large rectangle

Elastic

Large rectangle

5-6 Finish Small Rectangle's Short Edges, and Make Rectangle Into Tube

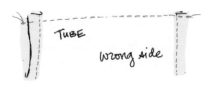

TUBE

wrong side

⑦ Join Headband and Tube

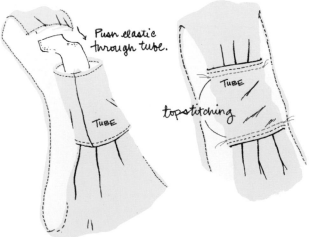

Push elastic through tube.

TUBE

topstitching

TUBE

GO-EVERYWHERE SHIRT DRESS

This dress works year-round. Make it up in a floral cotton lawn, and wear it all summer with the sleeves rolled up; or choose a dark chambray, and pair it with high boots in the winter.

I used a contrasting floral cotton for the underside of my collar and belt, which adds a bit of color and interest; but you can mix prints, combine a solid with a stripe, or just use the same fabric for everything. I also chose a navy blue cotton poplin with a bit of spandex—a fabric that's just a little bit stretchy will make a fitted garment much more comfortable to wear. If you do choose a fabric with some stretch, be sure to use a ball-point machine needle.

Finished Dimensions

NOTE: *Garment is meant to fit close to the body. Measurements below are taken from garment lying flat.*

Small: Bust 36", waist, 28"; hip, 38"; hem length from waist, 19"

Medium: Bust, 38"; waist, 30"; hip 41"; hem length from waist, 20"

Large: Bust, 40"; waist, 32"; hip, 43"; hem length from waist, 21"

Materials

2 ½ yards of 45"-wide lightweight woven fabric, preferably with a little stretch *(cotton lawns and poplins work best, but chambray, silk twill, or rayon also work well)*

⅛ yard of contrasting fabric *(for belt and collar)*

3 yards of 1"-wide fusible tape *(buy single-, not double-sided, fusible tape; if you can't find this tape, cut piece of fusible interfacing to match belt's width and length)*

16" of 1½"-wide double-folded bias tape made from dress fabric *(see page 152 for making bias tape)*

Ball-point machine needle for fabric with stretch or universal needle for non-stretch fabric

Hand-sewing needle

8 buttons *(between ¾"-⅞" in diameter)*

Water-soluble fabric-marking pen

Small fabric scissors

Point turner

Go-Everywhere Shirt Dress pattern *(see pullout pattern sheet at back of book)*

Sewing Instructions

❶ Lay Out and Cut Patterns

Trace (see page 149) the multi-size pattern, following the lines for your desired size, and cut out the traced pattern. Fold the fabric lengthwise, and lay out the pattern, as shown in the Layout Diagram at right. You'll cut 2 Dress Fronts, 1 Dress Back, 2 Sleeves, 2 Collars (1 becomes the Collar Facing), and 2 Belts. Use a water-soluble fabric-marking pen to transfer all pattern markings, including the bust darts and buttonhole placements, to the cut pattern pieces.

❷ Sew Bust Dart

On one Dress Front, align and pin the marked sides of the bust dart, with the fabric's right sides together. Then sew the dart, backstitching (see page 153) at the beginning of the dart, and press the dart to one side. Repeat on other Dress Front.

❸ Finish Placket Edges

Apply interfacing: Cut a strip of the fusible tape the length of the placket on the Dress Front. Following the instructions on the tape's packaging, fuse the strip, resin side down, to the wrong side of the shirt placket ⅛" from the placket's raw edge.

Fold, press, and sew placket's raw edge: With the Dress Front still turned wrong side up, fold and press the placket's raw edge ⅛" to the wrong side over the edge of the interfacing. Then turn the Dress Front to the right side, and fold and press the placket's edge again, this time 1" to the right side. Finally sew 1" across the placket's top edge, ⅜" from the neckline. Repeat the entire process above to finish the placket on the other Dress Front.

❹ Sew Shoulder Seams

With right sides together and the raw edges aligned, sew the shoulder seams on the Dress Front and Dress Back with a ⅜" seam, and press the seams open (see page 155).

❺ Sew and Turn Collar

Match and pin the raw edges of the Collar and Collar Facing with right sides together, and sew around the outside edge with a ¼" seam. Then trim the corners; turn the Collar right side out, using a point turner to fully turn out the corners; and press the collar flat. Finally, edge-stitch (see page 155) the sides and top edge of the Collar.

❻ Start Attaching Collar to Dress

With the dress right side out and its front plackets still folded wrong side out, layer the Collar right side up over the dress's neck opening, aligning the Collar's raw edges with one edge of the unfolded bias tape and the dress's neck opening; and pin the aligned edges in place. Be sure to leave an extra ¼" of bias tape extending beyond each side edge of the Collar, as shown in the drawing at right.

Starting at the edge of the placket, sew carefully around the neck opening along the fold of the bias tape, backstitching at the beginning and end of the seam and removing the pins as you sew. Use small fabric scissors to cut a notch between the edge of the placket facing and the Collar, as shown in the drawing. Then clip the top corner of the placket to reduce bulk when you turn it right side out in the next step.

❼ Finish Attaching Collar and Turn Placket Edges

Turn front edges of placket right side out, capturing ends of bias tape inside placket. Press placket in place and then bias tape around neck seam, capturing the collar's raw edges and neck opening inside tape's folds. Pin tape's edge in place.

Working from the wrong side, edge-stitch the tape, backstitching at the beginning and end of the seam. Topstitch the length of the inside edge of each placket facing, backstitching at the beginning and end of the seam.

❶ Lay Out and Cut Pattern

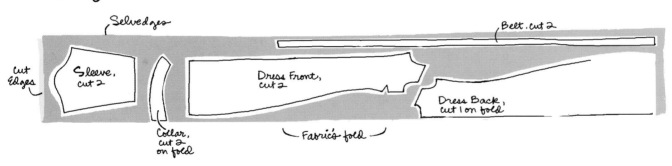

Selvedges

Belt, cut 2

Cut Edges

Sleeve, cut 2

Collar, cut 2 on fold

Dress Front, cut 2

Dress Back, cut 1 on fold

Fabric's fold

❷ Sew Brust Dart

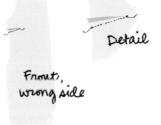

Detail

Front, wrong side

❺ Sew and Turn Collar

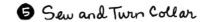
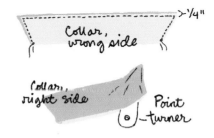

>1/4"

Collar, wrong side

Collar, right side

Point turner

❸ Finish Placket Edges

Front, wrong side

1/2"

Interfacing

Interfacing

1"

>3/8"

Dress Front, right side

❻ Start Attaching Collar to Dress

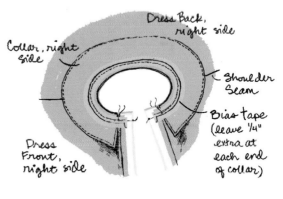

Dress Back, right side

Collar, right side

Shoulder Seam

Bias tape (leave 1/4" extra at each end of collar)

Dress Front, right side

Cut notch in dress front between placket and collar

Clip corner to reduce bulk.

❹ Sew Shoulder Seams

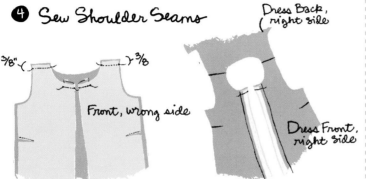

3/8"

3/8

Front, wrong side

Dress Back, right side

Dress Front, right side

❼ Finish Attaching Collar and Turn Placket Edges

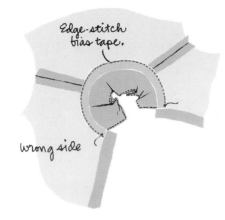

Edge-stitch bias tape.

wrong side

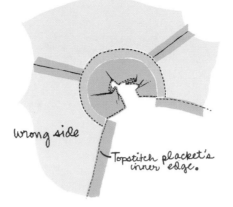

wrong side

Topstitch placket's inner edge.

❽ Sew Side Seams

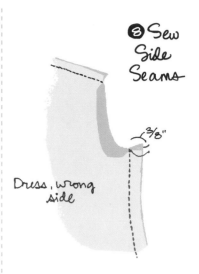

3/8"

Dress, wrong side

❾ Baste-stitch Sleeve's Shoulder

Dots transferred from pattern

Baste-stitch between dots.

❿ Sew Sleeve Seam

3/8"

Sleeve, wrong side

⓫ Sew Armhole Seam

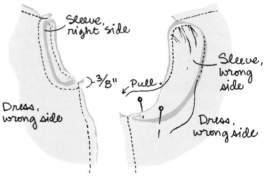

Sleeve, right side

Sleeve, wrong side

3/8"

Pull

Dress, wrong side

Dress, wrong side

Gently pull basting stitches and shape shoulder as you fit it into armhole

⓯ Make Belt

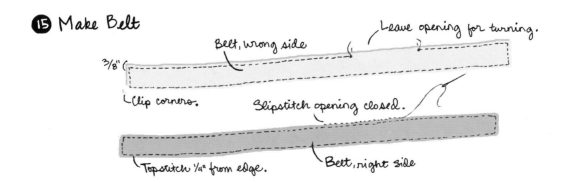

Belt, wrong side

Leave opening for turning.

3/8"

Clip corners.

Slipstitch opening closed.

Topstitch 1/4" from edge.

Belt, right side

❽ Sew Side Seams

With right sides together, align, pin, and sew the dress's side seams with a ⅜" seam, backstitching at the beginning and end of the seams. Then press the seams open (see page 155).

❾ Baste-Stitch Sleeve's Shoulder

Baste-stitch (see page 154) the top edge of each Sleeve between the dots you transferred in Step 1 from the pattern to the cut Sleeves.

❿ Sew Sleeve Seam

With right sides together and the Sleeve's long edges aligned, sew the Sleeve together with a ⅜" seam.

⓫ Sew Armhole Seam

With the dress turned wrong side out and the Sleeve turned right side out, place the Sleeve inside the armhole, matching up the edges of the Sleeve and dress's armhole and aligning the seam on both pieces. Gently pull the basting stitches on the Sleeve's shoulder to create roundness at the shoulder and fit the Sleeve into the armhole opening. Pin the aligned edges in place.

Sew the armhole with a ⅜" seam, backstitching at the beginning and end of the seam. Use the narrow end of your ironing board to "round" and shape the Sleeve's shoulder, and press the shoulder seam to one side (see page 155), toward the bodice.

⓬ Mark and Sew Buttonholes

Turn the dress right side out, and press both front plackets. Before trying to make buttonholes, read "Making Buttonholes" on page 156, and practice making a few on scrap fabric that you've interfaced, folded, and pressed to approximate the weight of the front placket. The interfacing that you fused inside the placket will help to make the buttonholes look flat and clean.

⓭ Attach Buttons

Attach your buttons using a hand-sewing needle following the instructions on page 157.

⓮ Mark and Sew Hem and Sleeve Hems

This dress looks best when its hem hits just above the wearer's knee. Try your dress on, and mark this length with a pin on each front edge. Remove the dress, and use the water-soluble marking pen to mark 2½" below each pin to allow for the hem itself, and connect these two marks with a straight line. Then cut along this line.

Fold and press the raw hem edge ¼" to the wrong side, and then fold and press this edge again, this time 2¼" to the wrong side. Pin the folded hem in place, and then edge-stitch the hem's upper folded edge in place.

Try the dress on again and pin-mark the Sleeve length you want. Then use the water-soluble marking pen to mark 1" below the pins for the hem itself. Fold and press the raw Sleeve hem edge ¼" to the wrong side, then fold and press this edge again, this time ¾" to the wrong side. Pin the folded Sleeve hem in place, and edge-stitch the hem's upper folded edge in place. Repeat for the other Sleeve.

⓯ Make Belt

To make the Belt, place the Belt and Belt Facing with right sides together and the edges aligned. Sew the pieces together with a ⅜" seam, leaving a several-inch opening on long side for turning. Clip the corners, and turn the Belt right side out through the opening, using a point turner to push the corners out. Slipstitch (see page 155) opening closed.

PAJAMAS FOR EVERYONE

These pajamas are easy and fun to make for everyone in the family, and a great project for a beginning sewer. They look fantastic in bright stripes and are a true luxury in silk satin. I suggest making them in cotton voile for summer and in cozy flannel for winter. Poplin and sheeting work well for just about every day in-between.

Sewing Instructions

❶ Lay Out and Cut Pattern

Trace (see page 149) the pattern, following the lines for your desired size, and cut out the traced pattern. Then fold the fabric, lay out the pattern pieces as shown in layout diagram on page 78, and cut out the pieces. Use a water-soluble fabric-marking pen to label the cut front and back pieces of the pajama bottoms, as they look very similar.

❷ Sew Front and Back Crotch Seams

With the right sides of the fabric together, align and pin the edges of the left and right Pant Front pieces along the crotch seam, and sew them together with a ⅜" seam, backstitching (see page 153) at the beginning and end of the seam. Press the seam open (see page 155).

Repeat the process to join the left and right Pant Back pieces.

❸ Sew Inseams and Side Seams

With right sides together, match the Pant Front and Pant Back, aligning the edges, and sew them together at the inseam with a ⅜" seam, backstitching at the beginning and end of the seams. Press the inseams open.

Then align and sew the two side seams, backstitching at the beginning and end of the seams and pressing the seams open.

❹ Make Casing and Insert Elastic

Turn the pajama bottoms wrong side out, and turn and press the top edge of the pajamas ¼" to the wrong side. Then turn and press this edge again, this time 1" to the wrong side. Edge-stitch (see page 155) the upper edge of the double fold to make a casing for the elastic, leaving a several-inch opening at center front for inserting the elastic. Be sure to backstitch at the beginning and end of the seam.

Finished Dimensions

Kids Small/Medium:
Fits 21-24" waist

Kids Large/Extra Large:
Fits 24-28" waist

Adult Small:
Fits up to 30" waist and 36" hip

Adult Medium:
Fits up to 35" waist and 42" hip

Adult Large:
Fits up to 40" waist and 46" hip

Materials

Mid- to lightweight woven fabric: 1½ yards for kids sizes; 2 yards for adult sizes Small and Medium; 2¼ yards for adult size Large

All-purpose thread to match fabric

1 yard of ¾"-wide waistband elastic

Water-soluble fabric-marking pen

Hand-sewing needle

Pajamas for Everyone pattern *(see pullout pattern sheet at back of book)*

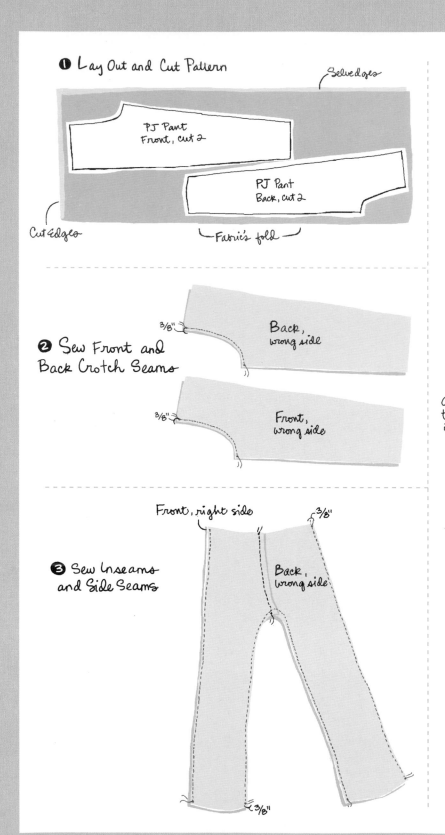

1 Lay Out and Cut Pattern

Selvedges

PJ Pant
Front, cut 2

PJ Pant
Back, cut 2

Cut Edges

Fabric's fold

2 Sew Front and
Back Crotch Seams

3/8"

Back,
wrong side

3/8"

Front,
wrong side

3 Sew Inseams
and Side Seams

Front, right side

3/8"

Back,
wrong side

3/8"

4 Make Casing and
Insert Elastic

Back, right side

Front,
wrong side

Attach safety pin
to elastic to guide
it through casing.

Zigzag-stitch
elastic's overlapped
ends, and
hand-stitch
opening closed.

Attach a safety pin to one end of the elastic, insert this end into the opening, and use the safety pin to thread the elastic through the casing. Try on the pajamas, and pin the elastic at your desired length.

Remove the pajamas, and add an additional ¼" to your elastic measurement. Then cut the measured elastic, overlap the two ends, and join them by zigzag-stitching across the overlap, backstitching at the beginning and end of the seam.

Using a hand-sewing needle, slipstitch (see page 155) the opening in the elastic casing closed.

✪ Hem Pajamas

Try on the pajamas again to determine the length you want, and mark this length with either a pin or with the water-soluble marking pen. Remove the pajamas, mark 1" below the marked length around each leg to allow for the hem itself, and cut along these marked lines. Turn and press each cut edge ¼" to the wrong side; then turn and press this edge again, this time ¾" to the wrong side. Edge-stitch each hem along the upper edge of the double fold.

LEFT AND ABOVE Lounging around the house on a Saturday morning is even more fun when everyone wears coordinating lounge pants.

Finished Dimensions

Small: Bust, 36"; length, 23"

Medium: Bust, 39"; length, 24"

Large: Bust, 42"; length, 25"

Materials

1⅝ yards of 45"-wide, woven, pre-washed cotton fabric *(or, if you want to make placket from contrasting fabric, use 1½ yards of main fabric and ⅛ yard of contrasting fabric)*

1 small button *(with shank or two holes),* ¼" in diameter

1½ yards of ¾"-wide double-folded bias tape made from blouse fabric or contrasting fabric *(see page 152)*

All-purpose thread to match fabric

Hand-sewing needle

Straightedge ruler

Loop turner

Water-soluble fabric-marking pen

Fabric scissors

Summer Blouse pattern *(see pullout pattern sheet at back of book)*

Choosing Fabric

I chose a cotton lawn from Liberty of London, but it will work well in any lightweight woven fabric like silk, cotton, chambray, or voile. I used a contrasting floral for the placket, bias edging, and button loops.

SUMMER BLOUSE

This blouse is the perfect cover-up for summer. It will protect you from the sun at high noon and from the cool breezes that threaten to peel you off the porch at the end of the day. It looks great matched with jeans for dinner with friends, or with shorts and a tan for just looking stylish.

Sewing Instructions

❶ Lay Out and Cut Pattern
Trace (see page 149) the pattern, following the lines for your desired size, and cut out the traced pattern. Fold the fabric lengthwise, and lay out and cut the pattern pieces as shown in the layout diagram on page 82. You will cut 1 Blouse Front, 1 Blouse Back, 2 Sleeves, and 1 Placket. Use the water-soluble fabric-marking pen to transfer the pattern's markings, including the bust darts, Placket placement lines, and basting stitch marks on the Sleeve's shoulder, to the cut pieces.

❷ Sew Bust Darts
Align the dart's two edges, right sides together, and machine-sew the dart together along the marked dart line. Press the dart's allowances up. Repeat to stitch the other bust dart.

❸ Sew Shoulder Seams
With the fabric right sides together and the edges aligned, join the Blouse Front and Blouse Back at the shoulder seams with a ⅜" seam. Press the seams to one side (see page 155).

❹ Finish Placket's Edges and Sew Placket to Shirt
Turn and press the sides and lower edges of the Placket ⅜" to the wrong side. Then, with right sides facing, pin the Placket to the Blouse Front, using the Placket placement lines you transferred from the pattern to the Blouse Front. Using a ruler and a water-soluble pen and working on the wrong side of the Placket, mark two straight lines down the center of the Placket, ⅛" apart and ending 1½" from the Placket's bottom point.

① Lay Out and Cut Pattern

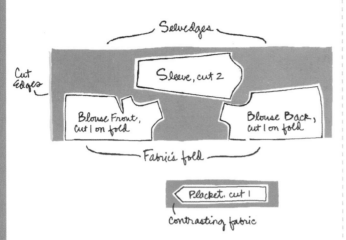

Selvedges

Cut Edges

Sleeve, cut 2

Blouse Front, cut 1 on fold

Blouse Back, cut 1 on fold

Fabric's fold

Placket, cut 1

contrasting fabric

② Sew Bust Darts

Align darts' two edges and sew dart closed.

③ Sew Shoulder Seam

Blouse Front, wrong side

3/8"

④ Finish Placket's Edges and Sew Placket to Shirt

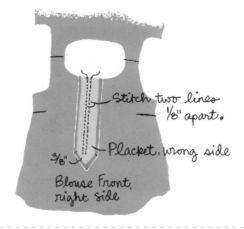

Stitch two lines 1/8" apart.

Placket, wrong side

3/8"

Blouse Front, right side

⑤ Cut and Turn Placket to Blouse's Wrong Side

Cut between sewn lines and notch bottom corners.

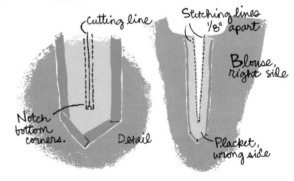

Cutting line

Stitching lines 1/8" apart

Blouse, right side

Notch bottom corners.

Detail

Placket, wrong side

⑥ Begin Binding Neck Opening With Bias Tape

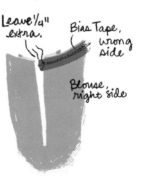

Leave 1/4" extra.

Bias Tape, wrong side

Blouse, right side

82

Beginning at the Placket's top edge, sew down to the bottom of one line. Then, with the needle down, lift the presser foot, and turn the Blouse Front 90 degrees. Lower the presser foot and take one or two stitches to get to the second marked line. Then, again with the needle down, lift the presser foot, turn the Blouse Front another 90 degrees, lower the presser foot, and sew back up to the top of the second line.

⑤ Cut and Turn Placket to Blouse's Wrong Side

Using your fabric scissors, cut a straight line between the two stitching lines, making a small notch at the base of the opening, as shown in the drawing at left. Turn the Placket to the inside of your blouse, and press the folded Placket in place.

⑥ Begin Binding Neck Opening with Bias Tape

Align and pin the double-folded bias tape around the entire neck edge, matching the top edge of the bias to the neck opening's raw edge. Leave ¼" length of excess bias tape at each end of the neck opening. Then use the crease in the folded bias as a guide for sewing, removing the pins as you sew.

⑦ Make Neckline Loop, and Finish Binding Neck Opening

Make spaghetti-strap loop: To make a 3" spaghetti strap for a button loop at the front neckline, cut a piece of Placket fabric 1" x 3". Fold the fabric rectangle lengthwise, with right sides together and the edges aligned, and sew the long raw edges together with a ⅜" seam. Use a loop turner (see page 152) to turn the spaghetti strap tube right side out (the tube's seam allowances will fill and round out the tube).

Sew loop in place: Tie together the thread tails emerging from each end of the tube to make a loop. Then fold in the raw edge of the bias tape extending from the right edge of the neck opening, and position and pin the loop's raw ends over the tape's folded raw edge, tucking these ends inside the tape's bottom folded edge sewn to the neck opening. Then fold the tape's upper edge to the wrong side of the neck opening, and press and pin the folded tape in place. Edge-stitch (see page 155) all four edges of the tape, sewing around the entire neckline, securing the loop on one short end, and backstitching (see page 153) at the beginning and end of the seam.

⑧ Topstitch Placket's Outside Edges

Turn the Placket right side out by folding its edges to the wrong side of the Blouse Front. Carefully pin the Placket's edges in place to the Blouse Front, and topstitch around the Placket's outside edge.

⑨ Sew Sleeve Seams

Baste-stitch (see page 154) the Sleeve's shoulder with two rows of stitches ⅛" apart between the baste-stitching marks you transferred to the cut Sleeves in Step 1. Gently pull the thread tails on the two rows of baste-stitching to draw up and round the shoulder; then press the rounded shoulder on the short end of the iron board to finish shaping it.

Fold one Sleeve with right sides together so that its long edges are aligned. Pin and sew these edges together with a ⅜" seam, removing the pins as you sew.

Repeat the process above for shaping and sewing the second Sleeve.

⑩ Sew Blouse's Side Seams

With right sides together, match and pin the Shirt Front's and Shirt Back's side edges. Sew the sides together with a ⅜" seam, and press the seams open (see page 155).

7 Make Neckline Loop, and Finish Binding Neck Opening

3/8"

Loop, wrong side

Loop, right side

Turn with loop turner.

Tie thread tails to make loop.

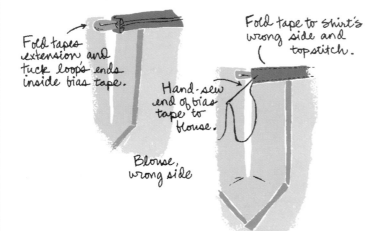

Fold tape's extension and tuck loop's ends inside bias tape.

Fold tape to shirt's wrong side and topstitch.

Hand-sew end of bias tape to blouse.

Blouse, wrong side

8 Topstitch Placket's Outside Edges

Topstitching anchors placket

Blouse Front, right side

9 Sew Sleeve Seams

Baste-stitch two rows, 1/8" apart.

Sleeve, wrong side

3/8"

11 Sew Armhole Seams

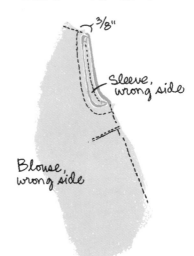

3/8"

Sleeve, wrong side

Blouse, wrong side

14 Sew on Button and Partially Close Seam

Hand-sew button and placket.

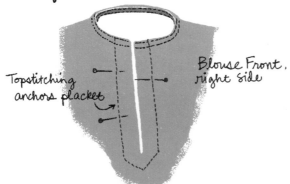

⑪ Sew Armhole Seams

Turn both Sleeves right side out, leaving the body wrong side out. Put the Sleeves inside the blouse, with the right sides together and the body's side seams aligned with the Sleeves' seams. Align and pin the edges of the top of each Sleeve and each Sleeve opening in place, and sew the two edges together with a ⅜" seam, removing the pins as you sew.

⑫ Hem Sleeves

Hem each Sleeve by turning and pressing its bottom edge, first ¼" to the wrong side, and then turning and pressing this edge again 1-2" to the wrong side, depending on your desired Sleeve-hem length. (This blouse looks best when the Sleeve hem hits at the base of your thumb when your arm rests at your side.) Then topstitch the upper edge of the double-folded hem in place.

⑬ Hem Blouse

Determine the best hem length for your blouse by trying it on and pinning the hem at various lengths. I have found that a hem that grazes the top of the hip bone flatters most body types. Once you've determined your best length, mark this length at various points with the water-soluble pen. Then add 1½" below these marks for the hem itself, connect the marks with a straightedge to create the cutting line for your hem, and cut along the marked hemline. Turn and press the hem's raw edge ¼" to the wrong side, and then turn and press this edge again to the wrong side, this time 1¾". A wide hem like this will add body to the bottom of your blouse.

⑭ Sew on Button and Partly Close Placket

Sew your button (see page 157) at the top left edge of the neck opening. Use a hand-sewing needle to slipstitch (see page 155) closed the opening of the lower Placket to your desired length. A good rule of thumb is that the Placket should not dip below the center front of your bra. For a braver plunge, consider adding more buttons and button loops along the Placket's edges.

TRAPEZE SUNDRESS

The secret to this flattering dress is simple: Its widely set straps play up a tan upper chest and shoulders, and its long lines extending from the bodice elongate your legs, especially when the hemline hits the narrowest part of your thigh. This dress is perfect for a picnic, barbecue, or pool or beach day. Its deep pockets are utterly suited for a quick trip to the snack bar, and its wide straps conceal bra or swimsuit straps.

Sewing Instructions

❶ Lay Out and Cut Pattern

Trace (see page 149) the multi-size pattern, following the lines for your desired size, and cut out the traced pattern. Then lay out the pattern pieces as shown in the Layout Diagram on page 88, and cut 1 Dress Front on the fold, 1 Dress Back on the fold, 2 Bodice Fronts (1 will become the Bodice Front Facing), and 2 Bodice Backs (1 will become the Bodice Back Facing), 2 Straps, 2 Strap Facings, 2 Pockets, and 2 Pocket Facings. Using the water-soluble marking pen, transfer the pattern markings for the Pocket placement, Strap placement, and box pleats to the Dress Front and Dress Back.

❷ Join Straps and Facings

With your machine set to a medium stitch length and with the fabrics' right sides together, join the Strap and Strap Facing with a ⅜" seam. Turn the Strap right side out, press it, and topstitch each long side ¼" from the edge. Then add three more decorative lines of topstitching, one down the center of the strap and two more equidistant from the center and topstitching lines.

❸ Attach Pockets

With right sides together, sew one Pocket to each side of the Dress Front, positioning the Pocket on the placement lines you transferred from the pattern piece. Repeat the process to sew the Pocket Facings to the Dress Back. Press the seams open, so that the pocket sits away from the skirt.

❹ Join Dress Front and Back

With right sides facing, sew the Dress Front and Dress Back together with a ⅜" seam, stitching around the outside edge of pockets as you sew.

Using the box-pleat guidelines you transferred from the pattern pieces, fold, pin, and press two box pleats in the Dress Front and Dress Back.

Finished Dimensions

Small: Bust, 36"; hem length from underarm, 26"

Medium: Bust, 38"; hem length from underarm, 27"

Large: Bust, 40"; hem length from underarm, 28"

Materials

2 ½ yards of lightweight woven fabric

All-purpose thread to match fabric

Hand-sewing needle

Water-soluble fabric-marking pen

Trapeze Sundress pattern (see pullout pattern sheet at back of book)

Choosing Fabric

Be sure to use a fabric that has a bit of body, like a voile or soft poplin. Indian cotton, cotton gauze, or double gauze (a very popular fabric from Japan) will work beautifully, too, as will a woven silk. Be sure to use the right needle when sewing with these fabrics—a microtex/sharp needle for the lightweight voiles and gauzes and a universal needle for cotton poplin.

1 Lay Out and Cut Pattern

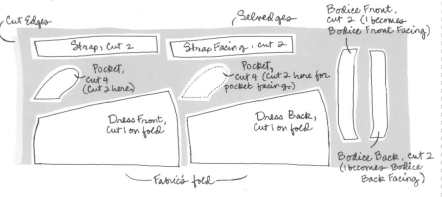

Cut Edges

Selvedges

Bodice Front, cut 2 (1 becomes Bodice Front Facing)

Strap, cut 2

Strap Facing, cut 2

Pocket, cut 4 (Cut 2 here)

Pocket, cut 4 (cut 2 here for pocket facing)

Dress Front, Cut 1 on fold

Dress Back, Cut 1 on fold

Bodice Back, cut 2 (1 becomes Bodice Back Facing)

Fabric's fold

2 Join Straps and Facing

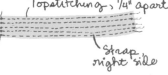

3/8 Strap, wrong side

Topstitching, 1/4" apart

Strap right side

3 Attach Pockets

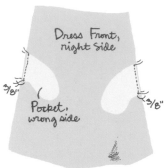

Dress Front, right side

3/8"

Pocket, wrong side

3/8"

4 Join Dress Front and Back

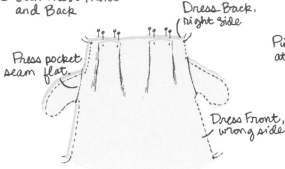

Dress Back, right side

Press pocket seam flat.

Pin boxed pleats at marked locations.

Detail

Dress Front, wrong side

5 Join Front and Back to Bodice and Bodice Facings

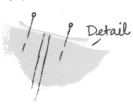

Bodice Back, right side

Bodice Front Facing, wrong side

3/8"

3/8"

Bodice Front, wrong side

Fold up 1/4"

7 Join Bodice and Dress

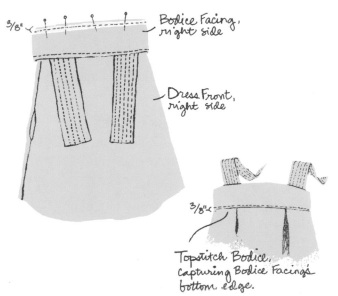

3/8"

Bodice Facing, right side

Dress Front, right side

3/8"

Topstitch Bodice, capturing Bodice Facing's bottom edge.

6 Attach Straps to Bodice Front

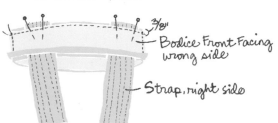

3/8"

Bodice Front Facing wrong side

Strap, right side

88

5 Join Front and Back of Bodice and Bodice Facings

With the right sides together, sew the Bodice Front to the Bodice Back at the side seams with a ⅜" seam. Repeat with the Bodice Front Facing and Bodice Back Facing.

Fold and press the bottom edge of the joined Bodice Facing ¼" to the wrong side.

6 Attach Straps to Bodice Front

Place the bodice, right side out, inside the bodice facing, wrong side out (so the two pieces have right sides together), and align and pin their side seams. Using the strap-placement guidelines you transferred to the Bodice Front, pin the straps in place between the Bodice Front and Bodice Front Facing, with the straps extending downward from the Bodice Front. Sew around the top of the bodice with a ⅜" seam, removing the pins as you sew. Turn the bodice right side out, and press it flat.

7 Join Bodice and Dress

With right sides together and the side seams aligned, match and pin the top edge of the dress to the bottom edge of the bodice (but not the bodice facing). Sew the bodice and dress together with a ⅜" seam, removing the pins as you go. Turn the dress right side out, press the seam you just sewed, and topstitch ¼" above that seam to capture the bodice facing's bottom edge.

8 Determine Back Strap Placement and Hem Length

Try on your dress; and, with the help of a friend, determine the strap placement on your Bodice Back. Then use safety pins to secure the straps in place at these points.

Next determine the hem length, and mark it carefully on each side seam with the water-soluble marking pen. Remove the dress, and mark 1¼" below your marked hem length on each seam, connect these marks, and cut along the marked line.

9 Attach Straps and Finish Bodice

Use a hand-sewing needle to slipstitch (see page 155) the straps in place on the Bodice Back. Cut off the excess straps 2" below the bodice, and topstitch five stitching lines around the bodice, as shown.

10 Hem Dress

Turn and press the hem ¼" to the wrong side; then turn and press the hem again 1" to the wrong side. Topstitch along the upper edge of the double-folded hem.

8 Determine Back Strap Placement and Hem length

Secure Strap with safety pin while hemming.

9 Attach Straps and Finish Bodice

Slipstitch Strap by hand.

Topstitch bodice.

Dress Back, right side

Finished Dimensions

Small: Fits bust 32-34", waist 26-28", hip 35-37"; skirt length, 20" from waist

Medium: Fits bust 35-38", waist 29-31", hip 38-41"; skirt length, 22" from waist

Large: Fits bust 39-42", waist 32-36", hip 42-46"; skirt length, 24" from waist

Materials

2 ½ yards of 60"-wide or 4 yards of 44"-wide silk jersey *(making top or bottom alone requires half this amount)*

1 ½ yard of ½"-wide elastic

Polyester thread to match fabric

Pinking shears

Small (28mm) rotary cutter

Ball-point needle, size 70/10 or 80/12

Hand-sewing needle

Point turner

Water-soluble fabric-marking pen

Saturday-Night Silk-Jersey Set pattern *(see pullout pattern sheet at back of book)*

NOTE: When sewing silk jersey, be sure to use a new ball-point needle to prevent snagging the fabric's delicate fibers; and also choose polyester thread, which has some give, rather than cotton thread, which tends to pop or break when stretched. Finally, using a rotary cutter will make cutting the fabric much easier since silk jersey tends to shift while being cut.

SATURDAY-NIGHT SILK-JERSEY SET

Both the top and bottom in this set are amazingly simple to make and are great basic pieces on their own. Pair the top with jeans and heels, or wear the skirt with a tank top and sandals. These pieces have a versatile, flattering fit, won't wrinkle, and are comfortable enough to fall asleep in on the ride home.

If you've never sewn silk jersey or worn this delicious fabric before, you'll be pleasantly surprised by its luxurious drape and the way it feels against your skin. It's no wonder that designer Diane von Furstenberg has built an empire out of this very fabric, her iconic "wrap dress," and the phrase "Feel like a woman, wear a dress."

Sewing Instructions for Top

❶ Lay Out and Cut Pattern
Trace (see page 149) the multi-size pattern, following the lines for your desired size, and cut out the traced pattern. Lay out the fabric and pattern pieces as shown in the layout diagram on page 92, and cut 2 Top Fronts (1 becomes Top Front Facing), 2 Skirts, 2 Ties, and 2 Tie Facings.

❷ Join Waistband Ties to Front and Front Facing
Set your machine for a zigzag stitch with a medium length and a narrow width. Align the Top Front and each Waistband with right sides together and the edges matched, and join the pieces with a ⅜" seam. Repeat the process with the Top Front Facing and Waistband Facings.

❸ Join Top Front and Facing
Place the Top Front and Top Front Facing with the right sides together and the edges aligned, and pin the edges together every 10-12". Zigzag-stitch the two pieces together with a ⅜" seam, leaving a 6" opening at the bottom of the waistband for turning the top right side out.

❶ Lay Out and Cut Pattern

Layout Diagram 60"- wide fabric

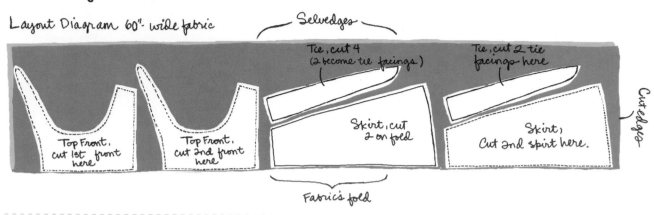

Selvedges

Tie, cut 4
(2 become tie facings)

Tie, cut 2 tie facings here

Top Front, cut 1st front here

Top Front, cut 2nd front here

Skirt, cut 2 on fold

Skirt, cut 2nd skirt here

Cut edge

Fabric's fold

❷ Join Waistband Ties to Front and Front Facing

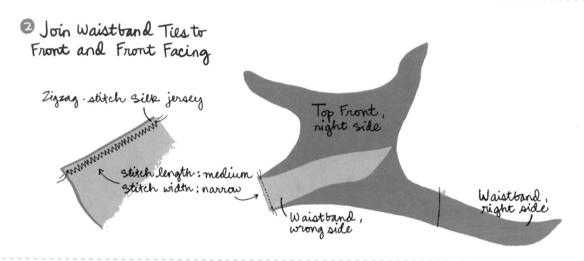

Zigzag-stitch silk jersey

Stitch length: medium
Stitch width: narrow

Top Front, right side

Waistband, wrong side

Waistband, right side

❸ Join Top Front and Top Front Facing

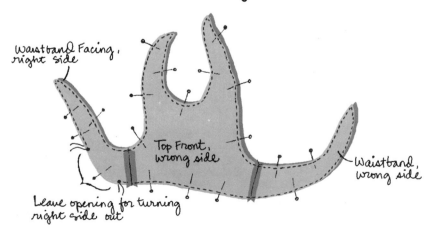

Waistband Facing, right side

Top Front, wrong side

Waistband, wrong side

Leave opening for turning right side out

❹ Turn Top Right Side Out

Trim all edges with pinking shears, and turn the top right side out through the waistband opening, using the point turner to fully turn out the waistbands' corners.

❺ Hand-Sew Opening Closed

After fully turning out the top's edges, press them flat, and use a slipstitch (see page 155) to close the opening.

Sewing Instructions for Skirt

❶ Join Skirt Front and Back

Place the Skirt Front and Back wrong sides together with the edges aligned, and join the pair at side seam with a French seam (see pages 97 and 99 for directions on sewing this seam).

❷ Measure and Join Waistband Elastic

Find your natural waist measurement by wrapping your elastic (without stretching it) around you, about 2" below your belly button or just above the top of your hip bone; then add ¼" to the measurement, and cut the elastic this length. Then use a zigzag stitch (set to a medium width and length) to join the ends of the elastic and make a loop.

❸ Attach Elastic to Waistband

With the skirt turned right side out, pin the elastic inside the top edge of the skirt's waist, as shown on page 94, positioning the elastic's joined edges at what will be the skirt's center-back point and stretching the elastic evenly as you pin it in place. Using a medium-length and -width zigzag stitch, sew the elastic to skirt's waist, stitching close to the elastic's top edge and stretching your elastic as you sew just enough so that the fabric lies flat while you stitch.

❶ Join Skirt Front and Back

Skirt Front, right side

3/8"

Seam allowance hidden in seam

Skirt Front, wrong side

3 Attach Elastic to waistband

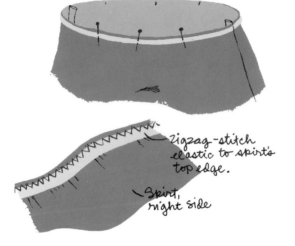

Zigzag-stitch elastic to skirt's top edge.

Skirt, right side

Fold stitched elastic to skirt's wrong side and zigzag elastic again.

Skirt, wrong side

Next turn the skirt to the wrong side, and fold the elastic to the wrong side and zigzag-stitch the elastic's second edge, stitching over the last seam you just sewed.

4 Hem Skirt

Because silk jersey will not ravel, the hem on a silk jersey garment is often left as a simple cut edge, or alternately the skirt can be finished with a narrow hand-rolled hem (see page 156). I like a simple cut edge for this skirt, and the key is to cut as clean an edge as possible. (Since a rolled hem requires a negligible amount of fabric, you could even decide after cutting the hemline whether to leave it unhemmed or finish it with a rolled hem.)

First determine the length that most flatters you (usually a hemline looks best intersecting a narrow part of the leg, like just below the knee). After measuring your desired hem length from the waistline, measure and mark that length on the skirt's side seams with the water-soluble marking pen or with pins. Fold the skirt in half, matching the side seams; lay it on a flat cutting surface, and smooth any wrinkles with your hands. Then, using the hem-length measurement and measuring from the waistline, mark several points along the hem. Use these marked points to cut a clean hemline.

Peaches and Basil from Warrups Farm

During the fall in New England, not a week-end is complete without a visit to a local farm stand. Warrups Farm in Redding, Connecticut, harvests my favorite peaches, which come into season just as the basil in their garden is at its most aromatic. I noticed how lovely the scents of these two crops blended, then created this delicious salad by combining them.

PEACH AND BASIL SALAD
Makes 4 servings.

2 large peaches

1 medium ball (about 16 ounces) fresh mozzarella cheese, very soft

About 20 large fresh basil leaves

1 tablespoon balsamic vinegar

¼ cup EVOO (extra-virgin olive oil)

1 cup cherry tomatoes, halved

Pinch of sea salt

Begin by cutting the end off of one side of a peach, parallel to the direction of the "slit" along its stem. Put aside the end, and continue slicing thin round layers of peach, about ⅛"-¼" thick, working on each side of the pit. Make similarly shaped slices of mozzarella. Now layer a slice of mozzarella with a leaf of basil and a slice of peach. Repeat, until your tower is about 4" high. Repeat 3 more times to create 4 towers. Whisk together the balsamic vinegar, salt, and EVOO. Drizzle the mixture over the towers, garnish with cherry tomatoes, and top with a rounded end of peach.

YARD-SALE WRAP SKIRT

This wrap skirt is inspired by the traditional batiked or block-printed Indian-cotton wrap skirts of the 1960s, though it has a slightly slimmer silhouette and a more flattering and modern hemline (meaning that it's a little longer than the typical '60s hem, which always ended awkwardly at the widest part of the calf).

This pattern will fit just about everybody, and can be easily made in one afternoon. I recommend a hand-sewn, rolled hem for its rounded bottom edge, which has a lot of curve and sweep, because the hem's wrong side inevitably shows and turning a curved edge twice for double-stitching on a machine is very difficult to do neatly.

Sewing Instructions

① Lay Out and Cut Pattern

Trace (see page 149) the multi-size pattern, following the lines for your desired size, and cut out the traced pattern. Lay out the pattern pieces as shown in the layout diagram on page 98, and cut 2 Front Panels, 2 Back Panels, 2 Overlap Panels, 2 Left Waistband Ties (1 becomes the Left Waistband Facing), 2 Right Waistband Ties (1 becomes the Right Waistband Facing), 1 Center Waistband, and 1 Center Waistband Facing. *(Note that, since all the skirt panels are cut from the same pattern piece, you'll have to move the pattern piece twice to cut all six pieces needed. And also note that the waistband ties and facings are different lengths because the Right Waistband Tie wraps entirely across the front waist to join with the short Left Waistband Tie.)* Using a water-soluble fabric-marking pen, label the right side of each cut piece.

② Join Skirt Panels

Position the two Front Panels' wrong sides together with their edges aligned, and join the pair with a French seam, which neatly encases the seam allowances. As shown in the drawing on page 99, sewing a French seam involves first sewing the seam with the fabrics wrong sides together, then trimming the seam allowances to ⅛", and then sewing the seam again, this time with the fabrics right sides together and using a ⅜" seam. Press the completed seam to one side (see page 155). Repeat this process to join the remaining skirt panels, positioning them as shown in the same drawing.

Materials

2 ½ yards of 45"-wide or 2 yards of 60" wide woven cotton, linen, or rayon

½ yard of contrasting fabric for tie *(optional)*

All-purpose thread to match fabric

Water-soluble fabric-marking pen

Point turner

Yard-Sale Wrap-Skirt pattern *(see pullout pattern sheet at back of book)*

Choosing Fabric

This skirt looks great made up in everything from the heaviest, most luxurious silk to the simplest quilting cotton. For added style, use a contrasting fabric for the waistband and tie facing, which will show nicely when the skirt is worn.

3 Finish Skirt's Side Edges

Finish the raw side edge on each end of the joined-panel unit by turning and pressing the edge ⅛" to the wrong side twice, then edge-stitching (see page155) the pressed double fold.

4 Join Waistband and Waistband Ties

With right sides together, align, pin, and sew one short end of the Center Waistband to the short end of one Left Waistband Tie. Repeat the process to join the Right Waistband Tie to the other end of the Center Waistband. Then repeat the entire process to join the Center Waistband Facing to the two Waistband Tie Facings.

5 Join Waistband and Waistband Facing

Turn the bottom edge of the waistband ⅜" to the wrong side, and press the fold. With right sides together and the edges aligned and pinned, sew the waistband and waistband facing together, as shown, starting at the bottom left side and backstitching (see page 153) at the beginning and end of the seam.

Clip the corner of each tie (see drawing at right), so the corner will turn neatly right side out. Then turn the waistband right side out, using your point turner to turn the corners out completely.

6 Join Skirt and Waistband

With right sides together and the skirt's center-front seam aligned with the center of the Center Waistband Facing, align and pin the Center Waistband Facing's lower edge to the skirt's top edge (remember that the skirt's ties are different lengths and hence will extend differing lengths from the skirt's side edges). Sew the skirt and facing together between the seam lines for the facing's ties.

Lay the skirt right side up, and pull the waistband into place so its pressed edge covers the skirt's raw edge joined to the waistband facing. Press the waistband's edge in place, and pin it through all layers. Then pin the edges of the waistband ties in place as well.

7 Topstitch Around Entire Waistband

Topstitch around the entire Waistband, sewing on the right side, starting from the end of one tie, stitching across the waistband's bottom edge first, and backstitching at the beginning and end of the topstitching. Press the completed waistband and ties.

8 Hem Skirt

Hem the skirt by hand with a rolled hem (see page 156). Steam-press the hem to flatten it.

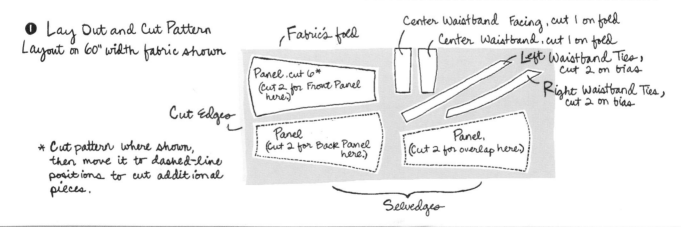

1 Lay Out and Cut Pattern
Layout on 60" width fabric shown

Cut Edges

* Cut pattern where shown, then move it to dashed-line positions to cut additional pieces.

Fabric's fold

Panel, cut 6*
(Cut 2 for Front Panel here.)

Panel
(Cut 2 for Back Panel here.)

Center Waistband Facing, cut 1 on fold
Center Waistband, cut 1 on fold
Left Waistband Ties, cut 2 on bias
Right Waistband Ties, cut 2 on bias

Panel,
(Cut 2 for overlap here.)

Selvedges

❷ Join Skirt Panels

Overlap

Overlap

Back

Back

Front

Front

Sewing French Seams:

1. Sew Panels with wrong sides together with 1/4" seam

2. Turn panels right sides together and sew with a 3/8" seam that encases seam allowances.

❸ Finish Skirts' Side Edges

Edge-stitching

❹ Join Waistband and Waistband Ties

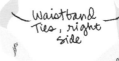

Center Waistband, right side

Waistband Ties, right side

5-6 Join Waistband and Waistband Facing, and Join Skirt to Waistband

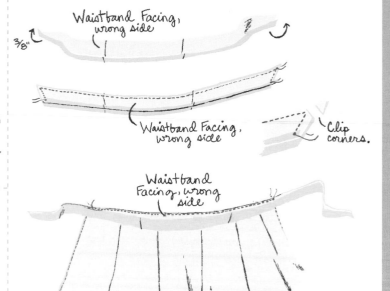

Waistband Facing, wrong side

3/8"

Waistband Facing, wrong side

Clip corners.

Waistband Facing, wrong side

Skirt, wrong side

❼ Topstitch Around Entire Waistband

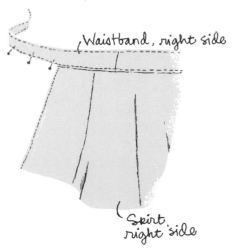

Waistband, right side

Skirt right side

Finished Dimensions

NOTE: *Garment's elastic waist is adjustable.*

Small/Medium: Fits bust up to 37", hip up to 39"

Large/Extra Large: Fits bust up to 43", hip up to 46"

Materials

For Dress

3 yards of 45"-wide lightweight woven fabric with lots of drape *(see page 145 for descriptions of fabrics with drape)*

All-purpose thread to match fabric

Elastic thread wound around an extra bobbin

Ball-point machine-sewing needle, size medium

Water-soluble fabric-marking pen

Straightedge ruler

Kimono Dress pattern *(see pullout pattern sheet at back of book)*

For Sash

½ yard of light- to medium-weight woven fabric with lots of drape

⅛ yard of contrasting, medium- to heavyweight woven fabric with lots of body *(for center-front facing)*

Double-sided fusible interfacing, 7" x 20"

All-purpose thread to match fabric

Hand-sewing needle

Point turner

Obi Sash pattern *(see pullout pattern sheet at back of book)*

KIMONO DRESS AND OBI SASH

I love projects that encourage mixing and matching fabrics because I love wandering around fabric stores looking for great combinations. This project mixes a versatile, comfortable dress with a sash inspired by the Japanese obi, which is traditionally worn over a kimono.

For the dress, look for a lightweight woven fabric with a lot of drape, like a silk satin, kimono silk, silklike rayon, or a synthetic blend. A rayon/linen blend will also work, as long as it has more drape than body. Avoid silk shantung and stiff cottons because the sleeves and skirt will not drape against your shoulders and hips, and you'll have too much fabric underneath the sash. Be sure to use a ball-point needle when sewing silky fabrics to prevent snagging them.

This sash should also be made of a fabric with lots of drape, although the center front facing can be made out of almost any type of woven fabric, and the stiffer, the better for a nice, flat fit in front that will not crease or fold when worn. Interfacing the center of the sash and sash facing is important since this is what will hold the sash's shape.

Sewing Instructions for Dress

❶ Lay Out and Cut Pattern
Trace (see page 149) the multi-size pattern, following the lines for your desired size, and cut out the traced pattern. Then fold the fabric, and lay out and cut the pieces, as shown in the Layout Diagram on page 102. You'll cut 2 Bodice Fronts, 1 Bodice Back, 2 Skirts, and 2 Sleeves.

❷ Join Bodice Front and Sleeve
With the right sides together and the long, straight edges aligned, join the right Sleeve and right Bodice Front with a ⅜" seam, backstitching (see page 153) at the beginning and end of the seam. Repeat the process with the left Sleeve and left Bodice Front.

① Lay out and Cut Pattern

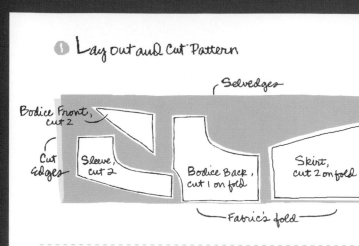

Selvedges

Bodice Front, cut 2

Cut Edges

Sleeve, cut 2

Bodice Back, cut 1 on fold

Skirt, cut 2 on fold

Skirt, cut 2nd piece here

Fabric's fold

② Join Bodice Front and Sleeve

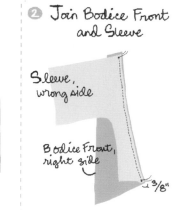

Sleeve, wrong side

Bodice Front, right side

3/8"

③ Join Bodice Front and Back

3/8"

Wrong side

2 3/8"

Bodice points

④ Finish Neck Opening

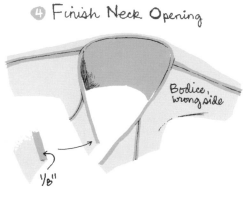

Bodice, wrong side

1/8"

⑤ Sew Skirt

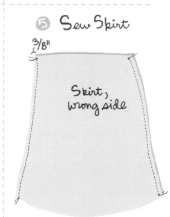

3/8"

Skirt, wrong side

⑥ Join Bodice and Skirt

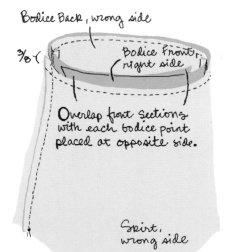

Bodice Back, wrong side

3/8"

Bodice Front, right side

Overlap front sections with each bodice point placed at opposite side.

Skirt, wrong side

⑦ Hem Sleeves

1/4" double-folded and edge-stitched

⑧ Hem Dress

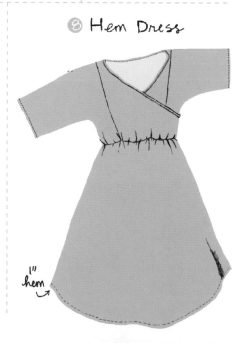

1" hem

🕒 Join Bodice Front and Back

With the right sides facing and the edges aligned, join the Bodice Front and Bodice Back at the shoulder and under-arm with a ⅜" seam. Press all the seams open (see page 155).

🕓 Finish Neck Opening

Finish the neck opening edge by carefully turning and pressing the edge ⅛" to the wrong side, and turning and pressing the edge again ⅛" to the wrong side. Edge-stitch (see page 155) the top edge of the double fold, and press it flat.

🕔 Sew Skirt

With the right sides together, join the Skirt Front to the Skirt Back at the side seams with a ⅜" seam, backstitching at the beginning and end of each seam.

🕕 Join Bodice and Skirt

With the skirt wrong side out and the bodice right side out, insert the bodice into the skirt (the fabrics' right sides will face together). Align the side seams; match up the skirt's top edge and the bodice's bottom edge; and carefully overlap the front sections, so the bodice front's bottom points align with the opposite side seam. Pin the aligned edges in place.

Change the bobbin for the one that you wound with elastic thread. Then join the bodice and skirt with a ⅜" seam, using a very narrow stitch length at the beginning and end of your stitching to secure the seam: After sewing a couple stitches at this narrow stitch length at the beginning of the seam, switch back to the regular stitch-length setting, and sew the seam; then a couple stitches before ending the seam, switch again to the narrower stitch length to end the seam. Press this seam to one side, towards the bodice, using lots of steam and heat. Then switch the bobbin in your machine back to the one wound with all purpose thread before continuing.

🕖 Hem Sleeves

Finish the sleeve hem by turning and pressing the raw edge ¼" to the wrong side twice and then edge-stitching the top edge of the double-folded hem. Repeat the process on the other sleeve.

🕗 Hem Dress

Try on the dress to determine your desired hem length. The most flattering length is at a narrow point on the leg—just above or below the knee or at the ankle. For most women, including those who are a bit curvy on top, the best hem length is just below the knee. For petite women and those with a small upper body, try hemming the dress just above the knee instead and wearing the sash tied high, just above your waist.

I always pin and press hems and try on the garment with shoes before actually sewing the hem. And when I make dresses from fine fabrics, I often take them to the tailor to be hemmed since it's inexpensive and comes out perfectly even and professional-looking every time—plus I get a second opinion on length.

To mark your hem length at several points, use a water-soluble marking pen or pins, and then remove the dress. Measure and mark 1¼" below the first marks to accommodate the hem itself. Measure this length along both side seams and mark, then cut carefully following the curve of the fabric's edge. Finish the hem by turning and pressing the raw edge ¼" to the wrong side; then turning and pressing the edge again, this time 1" to the wrong side; and edge-stitching the top edge of the double-folded hem.

1 Lay Out and Cut Pattern

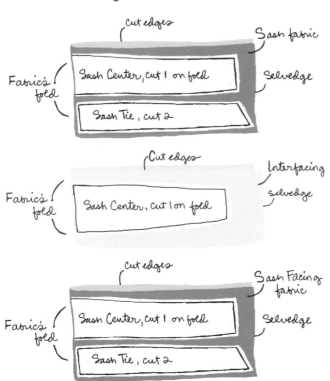

cut edges

Sash fabric

Fabric's fold

Sash Center, cut 1 on fold

Selvedge

Sash Tie, cut 2

Cut edges

Interfacing

Fabric's fold

Sash Center, cut 1 on fold

Selvedge

cut edges

Sash Facing fabric

Fabric's fold

Sash Center, cut 1 on fold

Selvedge

Sash Tie, cut 2

2 Interface Sash-Center Facing

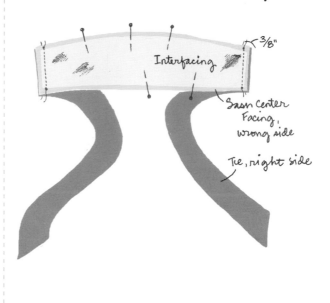

3/8"

Interfacing

Sash Center Facing, wrong side

Tie, right side

3 Join Sash and Facing

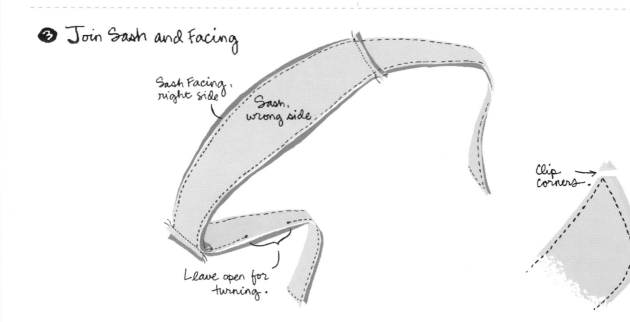

Sash Facing, right side

Sash, wrong side

Leave open for turning.

Clip corners.

Sewing Instructions for Obi Sash

❶ Lay Out and Cut Pattern

Fold the Sash fabric, Sash Facing fabric, and interfacing as shown in the Layout Diagram at left, and lay out and cut the pieces as shown. You will cut 3 Sash Centers on the fold (1 from the Sash fabric, 1 from the Sash Facing fabric, and 1 from interfacing) and 2 Sash Ties from the Sash fabric and 2 from Sash Facing fabric.

❷ Interface Sash-Center Facing

With the Sash-Center Facing turned wrong side up, place and pin the Sash-Center Interfacing on top of the fabric. With right sides together, align, pin, and sew one Tie Facing to one side of the Sash-Center Front Facing with a ⅜" seam, sewing through the edge of the interfacing as well. Then repeat the process to join the other Tie Facing to the other side of the Sash-Center Facing.

Then, with right sides together, attach the two Ties to each end of the Center Front with a ⅜" seam.

❸ Join Sash and Facing

With right sides facing, align and pin the sash and sash facing. Join the two with a ⅜" seam, stitching all the way around the sash but leaving a 7" opening in the middle of one tie for turning. Clip the corners.

❹ Turn Sash and Press

Turn the sash right side out through the opening you left, using the point turner to push the corners out completely. Carefully press just the sash's edges, pressing under the edges of the opening and avoiding pressing for now the center-front section with the interfacing. Before using an iron on the center front—which will immediately fuse the interfacing to the inside surface—use your hands to "press" and flatten the center front. When you've manually flattened the center front as much as you can, carefully apply heat with the iron to fuse and stiffen the center front of your sash.

❺ Close Opening by Hand

Use a hand-sewing needle to close the opening by hand with a slipstitch (see page 155)

Chapter 3

SEWING FOR KIDS

RUBY'S BLOOMERS

Bloomers are a bit of a throwback, I know, but they're a very practical, sweet addition to any little girl's wardrobe. This pattern for baby bloomers is a favorite project among my sewing students. They make an especially cute gift when given in sets of three, made from a mix of complementary printed fabrics or in varying sizes. Made up in white linen and monogrammed, they're an heirloom. Crafted in whimsical prints, they provide a complete outfit for the beach or a hot city day in the park. As you can see in this photo of our darling little friend Ruby, they look fabulous paired with a little bare belly full of lunch.

Finished Dimensions

6-12 months: waist, 15"*; thigh circumference, 8.5"; hip *(meant to fit over diaper)*, 24"

18-24 months: waist, 17"*; thigh circumference, 10"; hip, 27"

* You can easily customize the finished waist size when adding the elastic in Step 8.

Materials

½ yard of 45"-wide, lightweight woven, pre-washed cotton *(for notes on suitable fabrics, see Sewing with Elastic Thread on page 155)*

All-purpose thread to match fabric

Elastic thread

1 yard of ¾"-wide waistband elastic

Pinking shears

Water-soluble fabric-marking pen

Ruby's Bloomers pattern *(see pullout pattern sheet at back of book)*

Sewing Instructions

❶ Cut and Prepare Pattern

Trace (see page 149) the Bloomers pattern from the pullout pattern sheet at the back of the book, and cut out the pattern. Fold the fabric in half, matching the selvedge edges; lay out the pattern on the fabric, as shown in the Layout Diagram on page 110; and cut out the pattern. You should have two mirror-image pieces. Using a water-soluble fabric-marking pen, transfer the pattern's "Front Seam" and "Back Seam" labels to the appropriate seams on the right side of both cut pieces to keep them straight (they're easy to mix up).

❷ Sew and Trim Front and Back Seams

With the cut pattern pieces placed right sides together, align and pin the raw edges of the front and back seams, and sew each seam together with a ⅜" seam.

Using pinking shears, trim the raw edges of the seam allowances to ⅛" on the front and back seams to keep them from unraveling. Then press the seam allowances on the front seam to one side and the seams allowances on the back seam to the opposite side (see page 155).

❸ Sew and Trim Crotch Seam

With the Bloomers still turned wrong side out, align and pin the raw edges of the crotch seam. Sew the crotch seam with a ⅜" seam, and then trim its seam allowances to ⅛" with pinking shears.

1 Lay Out and Cut Pattern

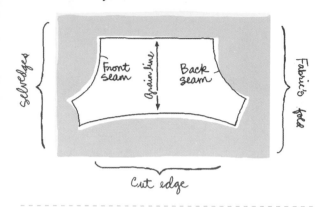

Selvedges

Front seam

Grain line

Back seam

Fabric's fold

Cut edge

2 Sew and Trim Front and Back Seams

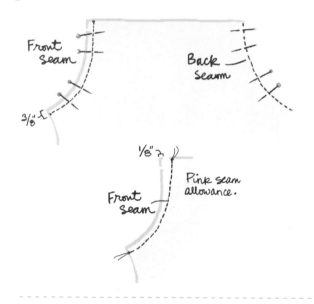

Front seam

Back seam

3/8"

1/8"

Front seam

Pink seam allowance.

3 Sew and Trim Crotch Seam

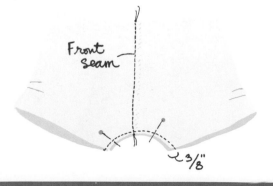

Front seam

3/8"

4 Hem Leg Opening

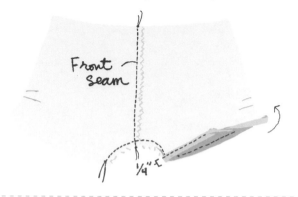

Front seam

1/4"

5 Sew Leg With Elastic Thread

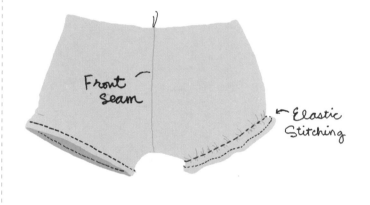

Front seam

Elastic Stitching

6 Turn Waistband for Casing

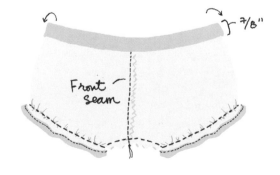

7/8"

Front seam

110

④ Hem Leg Opening

Turn and press the raw edge on one leg opening ¼" to the wrong side; then turn the folded edge another ¼" to the wrong side, and press the double fold. Edge-stitch (see page 155) the fold on its inner edge; then repeat the process on the other leg. Turn the Bloomers right side out, and press these edges flat.

⑤ Sew Legs with Elastic Thread

With elastic thread wound in your bobbin (see page 155), sew around each leg opening ¼" above your edge-stitching.

⑥ Turn Waistband for Casing

Turn the Bloomers wrong side out. Turn and press the top raw edge ⅛" to the wrong side; then turn and press the folded edge again to the wrong side, this time ⅞".

⑦ Edge-Stitch Casing

Starting ½" from the front seam, edge-stitch all the way around the folded edge, stopping ½" from the front seam, to create a casing for your waistband elastic.

⑧ Insert Waistband Elastic

Cut a length of elastic to match your baby's waist measurement plus ½" for seam allowances. To make it easier to thread the elastic through the casing, attach a large safety pin to one end of the elastic, close the safety pin, and then use it to guide the elastic through the casing.

⑨ Join Elastic's Overlapping Ends

Make sure that the elastic is untwisted in the casing, and then pull both ends of the elastic out of the casing a couple inches. Overlap the ends ¼", and then use a zig-zag stitch on your machine (set to its widest zigzag setting and a short stitch length) to join the overlapping ends, backstitching (see page 153) at the beginning and end of your seam.

⑩ Sew Opening Closed

Reset your machine to a regular-length straight stitch, turn the Bloomers right side out, and sew the opening closed, backstitching at the beginning and end of your stitching.

⑦ Edge-Stitch Casing

Front seam

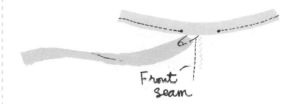

⑧ Insert Waistband Elastic

Front seam

Attach a large safety pin to end of elastic to make it easier to thread through casing.

⑨ Join Elastic's Overlapping Ends

Front seam

⑩ Sew Opening Closed

Front seam

SMOCKED SUNDRESS

My students at Purl Patchwork in New York City love this dress, in part, I'm sure, because it only takes an hour or so to make. (I actually whipped one up on the morning of my wedding for my cousin's daughter to wear as my flower girl.) The real beauty of this dress is its shape and fit. It's a great summer standby—casual made in quilting cotton and a little dressier made in linen or printed chiffon. It will fit for more summers than most cotton dresses, due to its stretchy nature and the fact that, in a pinch, it can work as a skirt. You can also extend its life by making it with shoulder straps that tie and can be easily adjusted or by leaving off the straps on the back of this dress, then tying the front straps, halter-style, around the wearer's neck.

Sewing Instructions

❶ Press Fabric's Top Edge

With the fabric wrong side up, turn and press the top raw edge ¼" to the wrong side, and then turn and press this edge again ¼" to the wrong side. Do not sew this folded edge yet; the pressed lines will be important guides later on. Unfold this edge, and lay the fabric flat.

❷ Mark Smocking Lines

With the fabric right side up, use the water-soluble pen and the quilter's ruler or straightedge to draw six (eight) straight lines, each ½" apart, across the fabric's width, beginning 1" below the fabric's top edge.

❸ Sew Smocking

With elastic thread in your bobbin and the fabric right side up, sew along your marked lines to create six (eight) rows of elasticized smocking. Backstitch or lockstitch (see page 153) at the beginning and end of each row to secure the stitching, and cut the thread before starting each new row (see "Sewing with Elasticized Thread" on page 155). Now you have a panel with elastic smocking across the top.

Finished Dimensions

Fits 12 months-size 4 (instructions are given for 12-month size, with measurements for size 4 included in parentheses)

Materials

¾ yard of 45"-wide quilting cotton or lightweight woven fabric, pre-washed (fabric should be lightweight enough to yield to elastic thread; test a small piece of fabric to see if it's suitable by following directions on Sewing with Elastic Thread on page 155)

All-purpose thread to match fabric

Elastic thread wound around an extra bobbin (see page 155)

Water soluble fabric-marking pen

Transparent quilter's ruler or straightedge

Measuring tape

2 yards of spaghetti strap, bias tape (sewn closed), or ribbon for ties, cut into four equal lengths

❹ Measure and Trim Smocked Panel

Using a spray bottle filled with water, generously dampen your "smocked" stitches. With a very hot iron set on steam and cotton, press the smocked area flat. You'll notice that the elastic "shrinks up" nicely and that your water-soluble pen marks disappear.

Using a measuring tape, take the chest measurement of the child you're sewing for, and with a water-soluble marker, mark the line from top of dress to hem. Before cutting the panel, secure the elastic threads by stitching across them at your chest measurement with a short, closely spaced straight stitch. Then trim off the marked, excess portion of your panel.

❺ Sew and Turn Smocked Panel

Fold the smocked panel with the fabric's right sides together, align the cut edges, and sew these edges together with a medium-width and -length zigzag stitch.

Turn panel right side out, press seam flat (with the seam allowances pressed to one side), and topstitch the seam allowances in place by stitching ¼" from the seam. This seam now marks the center back of your dress.

❻ Mark Strap Positions

Without stretching the smocking, measure 2" from the center-back seam in each direction, and mark these two points with your water-soluble pen. Then measure 6" from each marked point toward the center front of the dress, and mark two more points. These points mark where you'll attach the sundress's four straps.

Turn under the dress's top edge along the pressed creases, tucking the end of one strap underneath the folded edge at each marked point. Fold each strap up, as shown, and press the strap in place before edge-stitching (see page 155) the entire folded edge and the straps in place. Knot the other end of the straps to finish them.

❼ Hem Dress

Determine the dress's hem length by measuring the wearer from her underarm to just below her knee, and add 1" to this measurement for the hem itself. Measure and trim the dress to this length. Turn and press the dress's bottom raw edge ¼" to the wrong side, and then turn and press this edge again, this time ¾" to the wrong side. Finally edge-stitch the double-fold to finish your hem, backstitching at the beginning and end of your stitching.

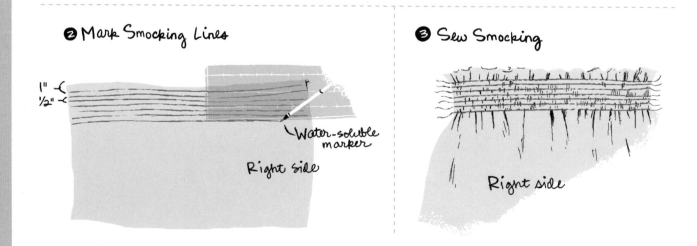

❷ Mark Smocking Lines

1"
½"

Water-soluble marker

Right side

❸ Sew Smocking

Right side

❹ Measure and Trim Smocked Panel

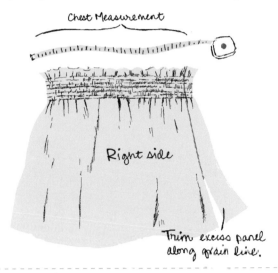

Chest Measurement

Right side

Trim excess panel along grain line.

❺ Sew and Turn Smocked Panel

Zigzag-stitch along raw edges.

Wrong side

Right side

¼"

❻ Mark Strap Positions and Attach

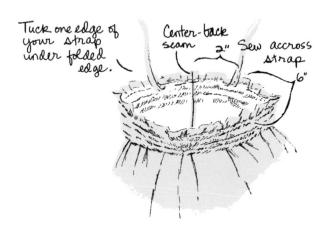

Tuck one edge of your strap under folded edge.

Center-back seam

2"

Sew accross strap

6"

❼ Hem Dress

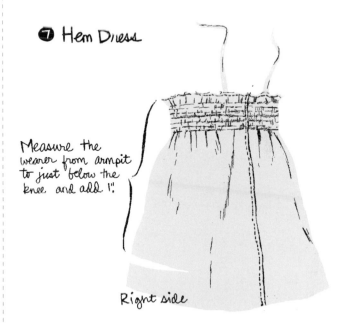

Measure the wearer from armpit to just below the knee and add 1".

Right side

12 months: chest circumference, 22"; neck circumference, 13½"; center-front length, 11";

Size 2: chest circumference, 24"; neck circumference, 14"; center-front length, 12";

Size 3: chest circumference, 28"; neck circumference, 15"; center-front length, 13";

Materials

¾ yard of light- to mid-weight woven fabric

All-purpose thread to match fabric and to match buttons

4 buttons, size 18-20 *(for sizes 12 months and 2; for size 3, 5 buttons needed. And for all sizes, it's good idea to have 1 extra button as replacement button.)*

Buttonhole foot or attachment for your machine

Point turner

Water-soluble fabric-marking pen

Hand-sewing needle

Kai's Shirt pattern *(see pullout pattern sheet at back of book)*

Choosing Fabric

Here's a trick I love: There's enough fabric in a man's shirt (one that presumably has a worn collar or stain) to make one of these shirts for a little boy. What a great way to re-use and remember.

KAI'S SHIRT

This might be just one little boy's shirt pattern, but its possibilities are endless. Made in Irish linen, it's fit for a party. Made in bright stripes or a fun print, it's an everyday standby. Made in a solid color and decorated with rubber stamps, fun buttons, or silk-screened designs, it's a conversation piece. My little friend Kai, who lives in a New York City neighborhood known by the playground set for its stylish toddlers, wears his version over a long-sleeved tee.

Sewing Instructions

❶ Lay Out and Cut Pattern

Trace (see page 149) the multi-size pattern, following the lines for your desired size, and cut out the traced pattern. Then fold the fabric, and lay out and cut the pattern pieces as shown in the Layout Diagram on page 118. You will have cut 2 Shirt Fronts, 1 Shirt Back, 2 Sleeves, 2 Collars (one becomes the Collar Facing), and 1 Pocket. Use the water-soluble marking pen to label each pattern piece and transfer the pattern guidelines for the pocket placement and button/buttonhole positions to the cut Shirt Fronts.

❷ Join Collar and Facing

Turn and press the bottom edge of the Collar ¼" to the wrong side. Place the Collar over the Collar Facing, with right sides facing and the top and side edges aligned; and sew the Collar and Collar Facing together, stitching over the fold in the Collar's bottom edge with a ⅜" seam. Clip the Collar's corners (see page 118); turn the Collar right side out, using a point turner to get the corners fully turned out; and press it.

❸ Prepare and Attach Pocket

Fold and press the Pocket's four edges ¼" to the wrong side. Turn and press the top edge again, this time ¾" to the wrong side, and edge-stitch (see page 155) this edge, backstitching (see page 153) at the seam's beginning and end.

Pin the pocket onto right Shirt Front following the transferred placement guidelines. Then carefully topstitch along both sides and the bottom edge of the pocket, backstitching at the beginning and end of the seam.

❹ Finish Shirt's Front Edges

Turn and press the front edge of the right Shirt Front ¼" to the wrong side. Then turn this edge again 1¼" to the right side, and sew along the top and bottom of this edge with a ¼" seam. Notch into the neck opening ¼", as shown; then clip the corner, and use the point turner to turn the front edge right side out, being careful not to push through the raw edge. Press the edge flat. Repeat the process with the left Shirt Font.

❺ Sew Shoulder Seams

Attach the Shirt Front and Shirt Back at the shoulders with a ⅜" seam, and press the seams open.

❻ Attach Collar

Baste the neck opening, ¼" from the edge. With right sides together and the edges aligned, pin the Collar Facing to the shirt; then sew the Collar Facing to the shirt with a ⅜" seam, removing the pins as you go.

Turn the Collar up, covering the raw edges of the shirt's neck opening and the Collar Facing, and press and pin this edge in place. Topstitch around the Collar and then along the folded placket edges, as shown.

❼ Sew Buttonholes

Using your machine's buttonhole foot or buttonhole attachment, sew buttonholes at the placement markings you transferred in Step 1.

① **Lay Out and Cut Pattern**

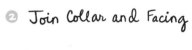

② **Join Collar and Facing**

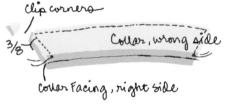

③ **Prepare Pocket**

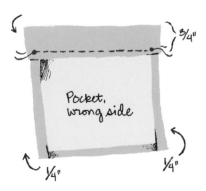

④ Finish Shirt's Front Edges

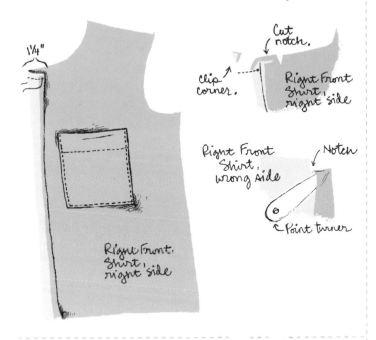

1¼"

Cut notch.

clip corner.

Right Front Shirt, right side

Right Front Shirt, wrong side

Notch

← Point turner

Right Front Shirt, right side

⑤ Sew Shoulder Seams

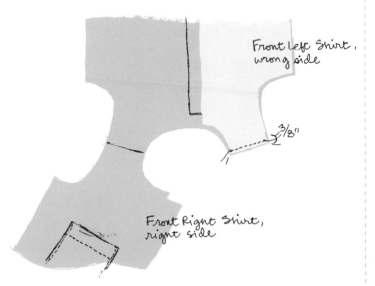

Front Left Shirt, wrong side

3/8"

Front Right Shirt, right side

⑥ Attach Collar

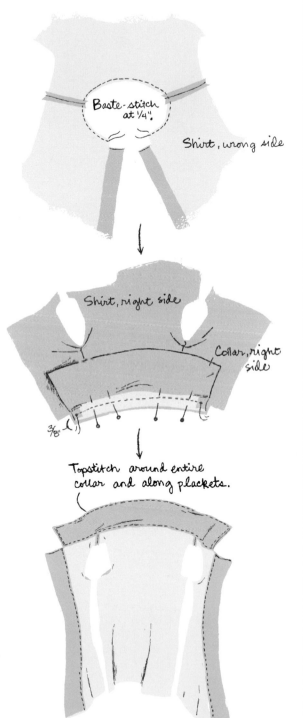

Baste-stitch at ¼".

Shirt, wrong side

Shirt, right side

Collar, right side

3/8"

Topstitch around entire collar and along plackets.

8 Baste-Stitch Sleeve's Shoulder

Baste-stitch (see page 154) the shoulder edge of each Sleeve, ¼" from the edge, leaving thread tails about 4" long on each end of the seam, so you can adjust the baste-stitching.

9 Sew Sleeve Seam

With the Sleeve's right sides facing and the long edges aligned, sew the long edges together with a ⅜" seam.

10 Hem Sleeve

Turn and press the Sleeve hem ¼" to the wrong side, and then turn and press the edge again ½" to the wrong side. Topstitch the double-folded edge, and turn the Sleeve right side out. Repeat the process with the other Sleeve.

11 Sew Shirt's Side Seams

With the right sides facing and the edges aligned, sew the shirt's side seams with a ⅜" seam.

12 Sew Armholes

With the Sleeve right side out and the shirt body wrong side out, push the Sleeve into the armhole, aligning the edges of the Sleeve and armhole as well as the Sleeve seam and the shirt's side seam. Pin the aligned edges in place (adjust the baste-stitching, if needed, so the Sleeve's shoulder fits neatly into the armhole). Note that the right sides of the Sleeve and the shirt's armhole should be facing each other. Then sew the armhole seam with a ¼" seam.

Repeat the process with the other Sleeve.

13 Hem Shirt

Hem the shirt's bottom edge by turning and pressing the edge ¼" to the wrong side, and then turning and pressing the edge again, this time ¾" to the wrong side. Topstitch the folded edge to finish the hem.

14 Sew On Buttons

Following the button-placement guides you transferred to the Left Shirt Front in Step 1 and using a hand-sewing needle and thread that matches the buttons (not the fabric), sew on the buttons, following the guidelines on page 157.

8 Baste-stitch Sleeve's shoulder

¼"

Sleeve, right side

9-10 Sew Sleeve Seam

Sleeve, wrong side

⅜"

½"

11 Sew Shirt's Side Seams

⅜"

Sewing with Children

In my home studio, I keep a small basket filled with wool scraps, buttons, and various trims. If young guests express an interest in sewing, I help them make a small stuffed toy to take home.

Children aged 5 and up can learn the basics of sewing using simplified tools: try threading embroidery thread through the large eye of a plastic children's sewing needle (these are not too sharp and are easy for small hands to grasp), and practice making simple stitches together on scraps cut from an old sweater. When a child has mastered a basic running stitch and expresses a desire to sew seams more quickly than can be managed by hand, they are ready to be introduced to a sewing machine.

In recent years, a good number of children's sewing machines have become available. Try www.hearthsong.com for wonderful new sewing machines (not toys; these are real machines!) and projects designed for kids. Many people collect vintage children's sewing machines, which are beautiful and fun to use. Some of these vintage machines are operated by hand crank, which can be a bit tedious but gives good control over speed. It can be fun to work together on a hand-crank machine, with one person cranking the wheel while the other guides the fabric.

Materials

For Blanket

½ yard of 60"-wide or ¾ yard of 45"-wide wool felt, cut into two rectangles, 9"x 24" and 17" x 24"

Poly-cotton or polyester thread in a color that contrasts with felt

Fusible interfacing, 8"x 8" *(select single-sided fusible, with removable protective coating on fusible side)*

Straightedge ruler

Transparent quilter's ruler

Water-soluble fabric-marking pen

Point turner

For Binding and Monogram

Strips of printed or patterned lightweight woven fabric, like quilting cotton, cut in following dimensions *(you'll need at least 4 different fabrics to make lively patchwork):*

Strip 1: 24" x 2 ¾"
Strip 2: 24" x 1 ¾"
Strip 3: 24" x 3 ¾"
Strip 4: 24" x 6 ¾"
Strip 5: 24" x 3 ¾"
Strip 6: 24" x 7 ¾"
Strip 7: 24" x 2 ¾"
Strip 8: 24" x 1 ¾"
Strip 9: 24" x 2 ¾"
Strip 10: 24" x 5 ¾"

Optional: Embroidery needle and embroidery thread for blanket-stitching monogram

PATCHWORK-TRIMMED BABY BLANKET

This blanket makes a wonderful gift for a new baby, especially when it is personalized with a brightly colored, patchworked monogram.

I made the body of this quilt with felted wool, but any felted or woven wool, alpaca, or cashmere fabric will work. To test a fabric, wrap your hand in it, and brush it against your neck. If it feels itchy, it's probably not suitable for a baby.

Sewing Instructions

❶ Join Wool Rectangles

Place the two wool rectangles together, with the right sides facing and one long edge aligned, and join them with a ¼" seam. Press the seam allowances to one side (see page 155), toward the larger wool rectangle.

Set your machine for a zigzag stitch with a medium length and the widest width possible (about ¼"). With the blanket wrong side up and the seam allowances pointing toward the left, position the fabric under the presser foot along the seam line, ¾" below the seam line's top edge. Start zigzag-stitching the seam from this point and continue down the seam's length, catching and flattening the seam allowances, and stopping ¾" before the seam's bottom end. (Starting and stopping ¾" from the seam line's top and bottom edges eliminates the bulk of the zigzag-stitching where you'll start binding the edge in Step 4.)

❷ Add Intersecting Line of Decorative Stitching

Place the blanket right side up, with the seam running vertically on the right side. Using a water-soluble fabric-marking pen, made a dot on each side of the blanket, 8 ½" from the top edge. Use a straightedge ruler to join these dots, drawing a line that intersects the existing seam.

Place the blanket under the presser foot, and, with the machine still set to zigzag, sew a decorative zigzag stitch from the blanket's left to right edge, following the drawn line. (There's no need to start and stop stitching ¾" from the edge, as in Step 1, since the zigzag-stitching alone will not add any bulk to the edges.)

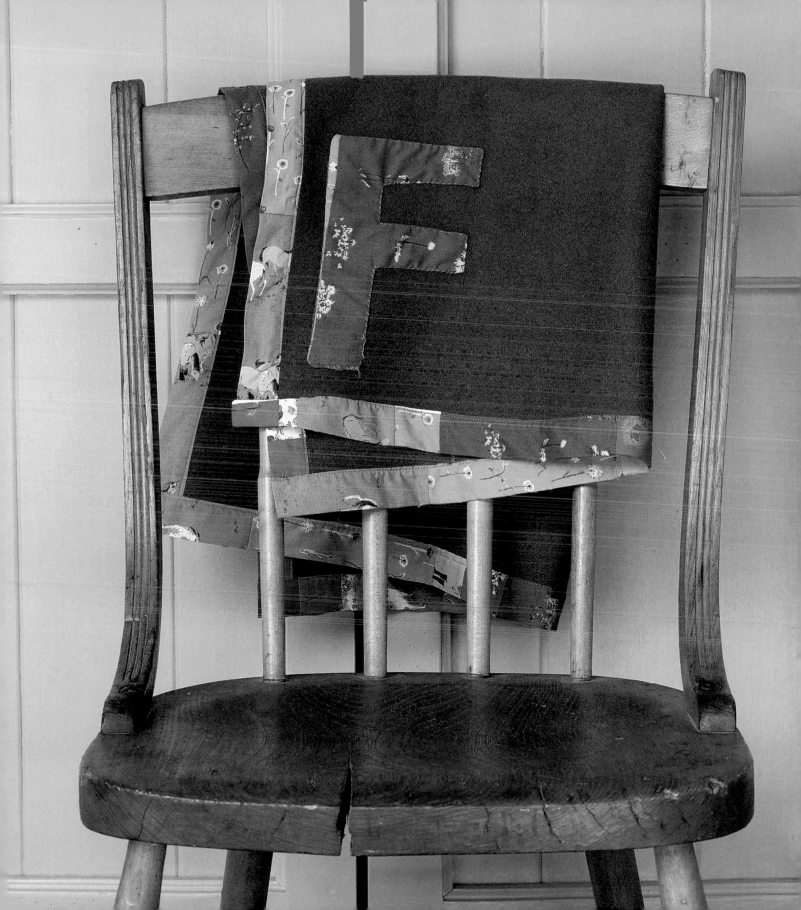

❶ Join Two Pieces of Wool

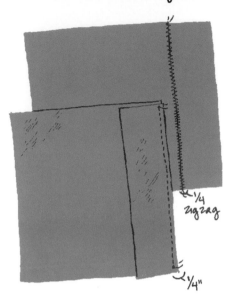

¼ zigzag

1¼"

Detail

¾"

← Start here.

Blanket, wrong side

❸ Make Patchwork Binding Strips

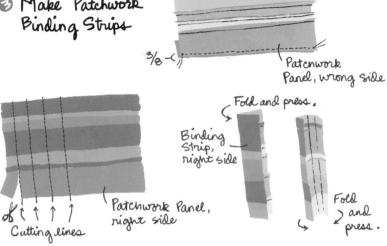

3/8 ⊣

Patchwork Panel, wrong side

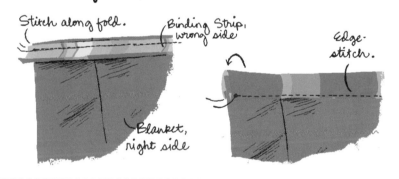

Cutting lines

Patchwork Panel, right side

Fold and press.

Binding Strip, right side

Fold and press.

❹ Attach Top and Bottom Binding Strips

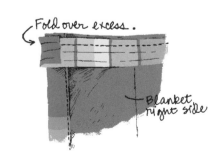

Stitch along fold.

Binding Strip, wrong side

Edge-stitch.

Blanket, right side

❷ Add Intersecting Decorative Stitch

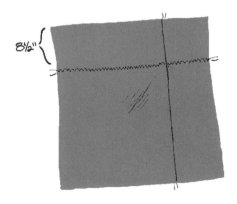

8½"

❺ Attach Remaining Strips of Patchwork Binding

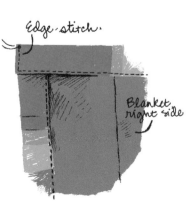

Edge-stitch.

Fold over excess.

Blanket, right side

Blanket, right side

❷ Make Patchwork Binding

Make patchwork fabric: First, reset your stitch for a regular straight stitch. To create the patchwork fabric for cutting binding strips (and later a monogram), begin by joining the fabric strips in their order in the Materials list: With the fabrics' right sides together, match and join one long edge of each pair of strips with a ⅜" seam, backstitching (see page 153) at beginning and end of each seam. Once you've joined all the strips, the patchwork panel will measure 24" x 32".

Cut and prepare binding strips: Press all the patchwork panel's seams to one side, toward the panel's top edge. With the panel laid right side up, use a straightedge ruler to trim the panel's left side so that it is even and perfectly perpendicular to the panel's horizontal seams. Then, beginning at the newly trimmed left edge, use a transparent quilter's rule to mark, then cut four strips of fabric, each 4 ½" wide.

Fold and press each strip in half lengthwise, with wrong sides together. Then unfold the strip, and fold and press each long edge so they match at the center fold. Put aside the patchwork remnant to use later for your monogram.

❹ Attach Top and Bottom Binding Strips

Unfold and align one edge of one patchwork binding strip with the blanket's top edge, with the fabrics' right sides together. Sew the blanket and binding together, stitching along the binding strip's first fold line and backstitching at the beginning and end of the seam. Trim the excess binding at each end, so the binding is even with the blanket's edges.

Fold the binding over the blanket's top edge, as shown in the drawing at left, using the existing fold lines as guides, and pin the second edge in place on the blanket's wrong side, placing the pins perpendicular to the edge. With the blanket right side up, edge-stitch (see page 155) the lower edge of the binding, removing the pins as you sew and catching the binding's other edge on the blanket's wrong side. Repeat this process with a second binding strip on the blanket's bottom edge.

❺ Attach Side Binding Strips

Lay one patchwork binding strip across one of the blanket's side edges, with the fabrics' right sides together. Center and pin the binding strip, so there's an even amount of excess hanging over each side. Beginning at the blanket's side edge, stitch in the binding strip's fold to join the strip and blanket.

Carefully fold each end of the binding even with the blanket's edge, and press the folded edge, being careful not to erase the binding's existing fold lines completely. Fold the binding over the blanket's top, pin it in place, and edge-stitch as shown, removing the pins as you sew and catching the edges of the binding on both sides of the blanket. Press the binding.

❻ Make Patchwork Monogram

Prepare monogram: Photocopy the letter of your choice from the pattern paper provided in the back of this book, enlarging the pattern by 300%. Lay fusible interfacing over your letter, with the fusible side facing down, and use your water-soluble marking pen to trace the letter's edges on the interfacing. Then lay patchwork-panel remnant from Step 3 right side up, place fusible interfacing with the letter drawn on it over fabric, resin side down, and pin the two layers together.

Sew monogram: Set your stitch for a short straight stitch. Position the two layers under your machine's presser foot, with the letter facing up; and drop your needle directly into your drawn letter at the start of a straight line, if possible. Stitching carefully, follow the traced line. If your letter has a corner, when you come to it, be sure to leave the needle down in the fabric before picking up the presser foot and pivoting the fabric to point in the new direction you want to sew. And also be sure to backstitch at the beginning and end of the stitching.

❻ Make Patchworked Monogram

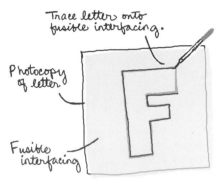

Trace letter onto fusible interfacing.

Photocopy of letter

Fusible interfacing

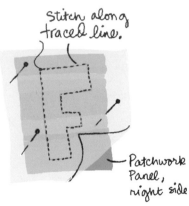

Stitch along traced line.

Patchwork Panel, right side

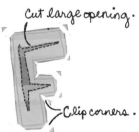

Cut large opening.

Clip corners.

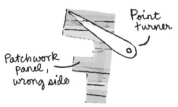

Turn letter right side out.

Point turner

Patchwork Panel, wrong side

Cut and turn monogram right side out: Cut out your letter about ¼" from the stitched line, and clip all corners, as shown. Then cut one or more large slits in the fusible interfacing (the number and placement of the slits depend on the letter's shape, as you can see in the drawing at left), being sure not to cut into the fabric below. Remove the fusible interfacing's protective backing, and turn the letter right side out through the slits, using a point turner to fully push each side into shape. "Press" the letter with your hands (not the iron at this point) so that each edge is even and fully turned out.

❼ Attach Monogram to Blanket

Lay and lightly pin the monogram on top of the blanket in your desired location. I placed mine 3" from both edges in the upper left corner, but you may want to place yours at the blanket's center or near another edge.

Carefully press the letter, which will fuse the interfacing and letter to the blanket. If you want, it's easy to hand-sew a slipstitch (see page 155) or a blanket stitch (see page 47) around the letter's edges, using an embroidery needle and embroidery thread in a matching or contrasting color.

❼ Attach Monogram to Blanket

Slipstitch or blanket-stitch.

Blueberry Mash for Baby

Weekends mean extra time for things like berry picking, and if your family lives close to the mountains of northern New England, late summer week-ends mean lots of fresh blueberries. This is good news for my little blue-berry crazy friend Allie, but bad news for her parents who aren't crazy about the way the berries tumble out of small hands and resurface later as mysterious stains on the rug. Allie's mom, Danielle, and I devised this simple little mash for Allie and her little brother, Will, who is also a big fan of blueberries, especially when they don't roll off his little spoon, which he finds maddening.

BLUEBERRIES FOR BABIES

1 cup fresh blueberries, stems removed
2 tablespoons vanilla yogurt

Place blueberries in a small food proces-sor, and pulse a few times until berries are chopped. Use a rubber spatula to spoon into a mixing bowl, and fold in yogurt. Serves two very hungry children, with a little leftover for the top of Dad's cereal.

HUCK FINN PANTS

These pants are a great baby/toddler basic and can be made from a variety of fabrics. I've used a soft cotton poplin in a bright stripe here, but I've also made them from linen and chambray for very lightweight summer pants and once even made them for a little boy from his father's old blue jeans. I've created an adjustable waistband by adding a button and buttonholes to a length of ¾"-wide waistband elastic, a great trick for assuring a pair of pants a long life. These pants look great, Huck Finn-style, with a little bit of ankle showing.

For extra flair, add topstitching in brightly colored thread—if your sewing lines aren't exactly straight yet, use a straight-edge and a water-soluble fabric-marking pen to make guidelines for the seams before sewing.

Sewing Instructions

❶ Lay Out and Cut Pattern
Trace (see page 149) the multi-size pattern, following the lines for your desired size, and cut out the traced pattern. Then fold the fabric with the right sides facing and the selvedges aligned. Position the two pattern pieces as shown in the layout diagram on page 130, and cut out 2 Pant Fronts and 2 Pant Backs.

❷ Sew Front and Back Seams
With the fabric's right sides facing, align, pin, and sew the two front pieces together with a ⅜" seam.

Use pinking shears to trim the seam's allowances to ¼". Press the pants' front open, pressing the seam allowances over to one side. Repeat the process to join the two back pieces.

❸ Sew Crotch and Side Seams
With right sides facing, match and pin the raw edges of the Pant Front to the Pant Back along the crotch seam, and sew them with a ⅜" seam. Press the allowances to one side, towards the front of the pants.

Finished Dimensions

12 months: Inseam, 9"; waist, 16"

18 months: Inseam, 9.5"; waist, 16.5"

24 months: Inseam, 10"; waist, 17"

Materials

¾ yard of lightweight, striped, pre-washed, mid-weight woven fabric *(like linen, quilting cotton, denim, or lightweight canvas)*

1 yard of ¾"-wide waistband elastic

All-purpose thread to match fabric

1 button, ½" to ¾" in diameter

Hand-sewing needle

Pinking shears

Huck Finn Pants pattern *(see pullout pattern sheet at back of book)*

① Lay Out and Cut Pattern

Selvedges

Pant Back, cut 2

Pant Front, cut 2

Fabric's fold

Cut Edge

② Sew Front and Back Seams

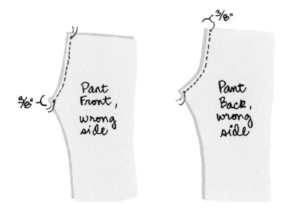

3/8"

3/8"

Pant Front, wrong side

Pant Back, wrong side

③ Sew Crotch and Side Seams

wrong side

3/8"

3/8"

④ Topstitch Side Seams and Inseams

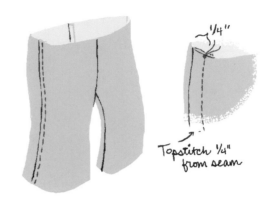

1/4"

Topstitch 1/4" from seam

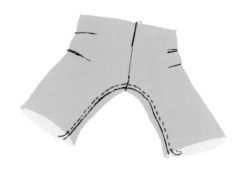

⑥ Hem Pants and Make Waistband Casing for Elastic

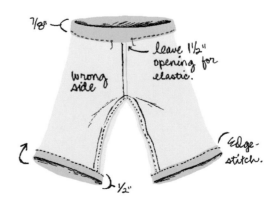

7/8"

leave 1½" opening for elastic.

wrong side

Edge-stitch.

1/2"

With right sides still facing, match up and pin the raw edges on each side of the pant leg, and sew them with a ⅜" seam. Press the two seam allowances to one side, towards the front of the pants.

❹ Topstitch Side Seams and Inseams
To strengthen the side seams and inseams, turn the pants right side out, and topstitch the seam allowances in place ¼" from the seam line. Be sure to backstitch (see page 153) at the beginning and end of each seam, and then press the top-stitched seams.

❺ Hem Pants
Turn the pants wrong side out, turn each hem edge ¼" to the wrong side, and press the fold. Turn each hem another ½" to the wrong side, press the double-folded hem, and edge-stitch (see page 155) the double fold.

❻ Make Waistband Casing for Elastic
With the pants still turned wrong side out, turn the top raw edge ⅛" to the wrong side, and press the fold. Then turn and press the folded edge another ⅞" to the wrong side. Edge-stitch the folded edge to create a casing for the elastic, starting and stopping stitching ¾" from the center-front seam to leave a 1½" opening for inserting the elastic.

❼ Sew and Insert Waistband Elastic
Measure the waist of your intended wearer. Add 3½" to this measurement, and trim the length of the waistband elastic to this measurement. Using the size of your button as a guide, make four horizontal buttonholes (see "Making Buttonholes" on page 156), at least ¼" apart, at one end of the elastic. Sew your button on the other end of the elastic (see page 157).

Attach a large safety pin to the elastic through the end buttonhole. Close the safety pin, and use it to help guide your elastic through your casing. Once you've fed the elastic entirely through the casing, remove the safety pin, button the two ends of the elastic together (making sure the elastic has not gotten twisted in the casing), and "snap" the waistband with both hands a couple times to get the elastic fully seated inside the casing.

❽ Hand-Sew Casing's Opening Closed
It's a good idea to use a hand-sewing needle to close the opening in the casing, so that little fingers don't reach into the opening and pull out the button or elastic. Make large basting stitches (see page 153) that can be pulled out when needed to adjust the elastic later.

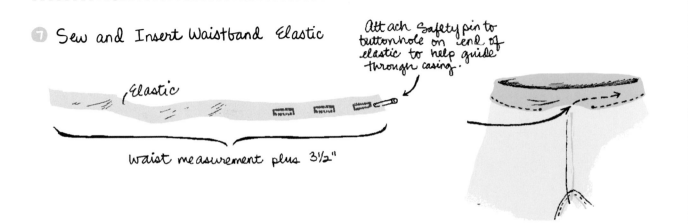

❼ Sew and Insert Waistband Elastic

Attach safety pin to buttonhole on end of elastic to help guide through casing.

Elastic

waist measurement plus 3½"

Finished Dimensions

NOTE: *Bust refers to widest part of girl's chest, regardless of her age.*

Size 2: chest circumference, 19"; length, 14" below bust

Size 3: chest circumference, 20"; length, 16" below bust

Size 4: chest circumference, 21"; length, 18" below bust

Materials

1 yard of lightweight woven fabric *(like silk shantung, silk organza, silk satin, silk faille, silk chambray, cotton poplin, cotton lawn, shirting, or linen)*

Thread to match fabric

Loop turner

Fabric scissors

Hand-sewing needle

Water-soluble fabric-marking pen

Straightedge ruler

Flower Girl Dress pattern *(see pullout pattern sheet at back of book)*

Choosing Fabric

When made up in silk shantung and tied with a sash, this dress becomes surprisingly fancy. Its length—best just above the ankle—adds formality, as do its thin straps. I also love this dress made up in washed linen, with a sash made from organza. The possibilities are endless.

FLOWER GIRL DRESS

When my cousins and I were small, we wore dresses like this one to our uncle's wedding. They were sewn especially for us by a local seamstress, which made us feel very important. In memory of that little dress, I made this one, which I hope will inspire similar happy stories.

This pattern works for girls aged four to eight or so, but once you've made one dress, you'll see that the pattern and construction are simple enough to make alterations for smaller and larger sizes.

Sewing Instructions

❶ Lay Out and Cut Pattern
Trace (see page 149) the pattern, following the lines for your desired size, and cut out the traced size. Fold the fabric, and lay out and cut the pattern pieces, as shown in the layout diagram on page 134. You'll cut 2 Bodice Fronts (1 becomes the Bodice Front Facing), 2 Bodice Backs (1 becomes the Bodice Back Facing), and 2 Skirts.

❷ Make Thin Straps
Use the fabric remnants from Step 1 to make thin straps for the dress by first cutting one rectangle 1" wide x 20" long. Fold and press the rectangle in half lengthwise, with right sides together and the edges aligned. Using a medium-length stitch, sew the long edges together with a ¼" seam. Using a loop turner (see page 152), turn the tube right side out to make a long strap. Press the strap flat; then cut the length in half.

❸ Join Bodice Front and Bodice Back
Place the Bodice Front and Bodice Front Facing together, with right sides facing, the top edges aligned, and one end of each strap positioned in between the two fabric layers on each side, as shown. Using a medium-length stitch, sew from Point A to Point B with a ³⁄₈" seam.

❶ Lay Out and Cut Pattern

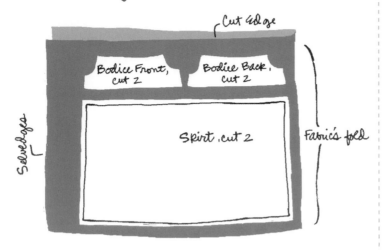

Cut Edge

Bodice Front, cut 2

Bodice Back, cut 2

Skirt, cut 2

Selvedge

Fabric's fold

❷ Make Thin Straps

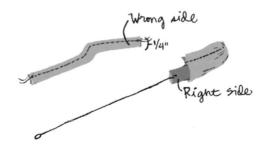

Wrong side

7 1/4"

Right side

❹ Prepare Bodice to be Joined to Skirt

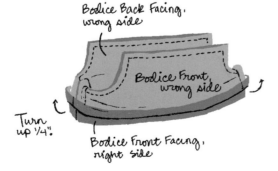

Bodice Back Facing, wrong side

Bodice Front, wrong side

Turn up 1/4".

Bodice Front Facing, right side

❸ Join Bodice Front and Bodice Back

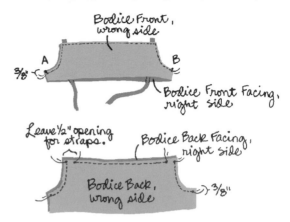

Bodice Front, wrong side

3/8"

A

B

Bodice Front Facing, right side

Leave 1/2" opening for straps.

Bodice Back Facing, right side

Bodice Back, wrong side

3/8"

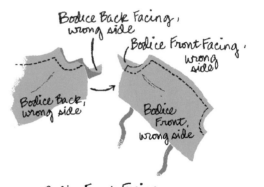

Bodice Back Facing, wrong side

Bodice Front Facing, wrong side

Bodice Back, wrong side

Bodice Front, wrong side

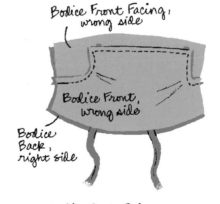

Bodice Front Facing, wrong side

Bodice Front, wrong side

Bodice Back, right side

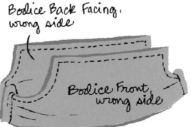

Bodice Back Facing, wrong side

Bodice Front, wrong side

Place the Bodice Back and Bodice Back Facing together, with right sides facing and the top edges aligned; and sew them together with a ⅜" seam, leaving ½" openings for inserting the other ends of the straps later.

To join the Bodice Front and Bodice Back, match and pin the faced pieces, which should still be turned wrong side out, at the side seams. Then stitch the sides together with a ⅜" seam, removing the pins as you sew.

④ Prepare Bodice to Be Joined to Skirt

With the Bodice Front/Facing unit still turned wrong side out, turn the edge of the Bodice Front (but not the Bodice Front Facing) ¼" to the wrong side, and press the edge. Turn the Bodice right side out, using a point turner to shape the corners.

⑤ Sew and Gather Skirt

Match the Front and Back Skirts, with right sides facing and the edges aligned, and sew them together with a ⅜" seam. Press the seams open (see page 149). Using a machine-basting stitch (or the longest stitch setting on your machine), sew a line of gathering stitches around the skirt's top edge about ¼" from the edge.

⑥ Sew Bodice Facing to Skirt

Pin the bottom edge of the Bodice Facing (but not the Bodice) to the top edge of the Skirt, with right sides together, adjusting the Skirt's gathers so they're evenly spaced and the Skirt fits perfectly inside the Bodice. Stitch the Skirt and Bodice Facing together, removing the pins as you sew. (Note that pressing the gathers flat before pinning and sewing the Bodice Facing and Skirt will straighten the Skirt's gathers and make them easier to sew.)

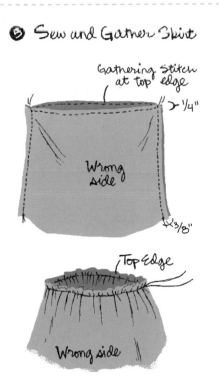

⑤ Sew and Gather Skirt

Gathering stitch at top edge

¼"

Wrong Side

⅜"

Top Edge

Wrong side

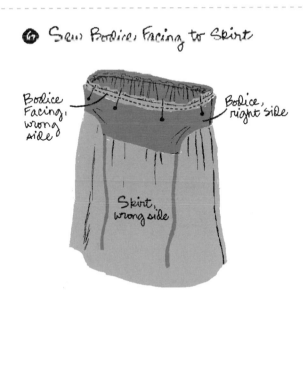

⑥ Sew Bodice Facing to Skirt

Bodice Facing, wrong side

Bodice, right side

Skirt, wrong side

7 Sew Bodice to Skirt

Turn the dress right side out, and place the folded bottom edge of the Bodice over the Skirt's top raw, gathered edge. Press this edge in place, pin it through all the layers, and carefully topstitch ⅛" above the folded edge.

8 Determine Length of Straps and Hem

Put your dress on its intended wearer, and determine how long the straps should be, adding 1" extra for a ½" seam allowance on each end of the strap. Insert the straps in the openings you left in the Back Bodice seam in Step 3, and pin them in place with safety pins (so you can remove the dress without removing the pins). While the child still has the dress on, also mark where the hem should fall with a safety pin at each side seam.

9 Sew Hem

Remove the dress, mark 2 ½" below each side-seam pin to provide for the hem itself, connect the new marks with the water-soluble marking pen and straightedge ruler, and cut along this marked line. Fold and press the hem edge ¼" to the wrong side, and then fold and press this edge again 2" to the wrong side. Pin the hem, and carefully topstitch along its upper folded edge, removing the pins as you sew.

10 Hand-Sew Back Straps

Using a hand-sewing needle, attach the straps to the Back Bodice by stitching closed the opening around each strap, sewing through all layers of strap and Bodice.

7 Sew Bodice to Skirt

Topstitch ⅛" above folded edge.

Right side

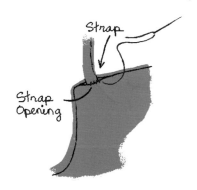

10 Hand-Sew Back Straps

Strap

Strap Opening

Weekend Indulgence

While for most of us weekdays do not typically include special meals and desserts, weekends seem to allow for a few more indulgences. This recipe is a family favorite. My uncle's mountaintop farm in Vermont once produced some of the most delicious maple syrup anywhere, and my grandfather would proudly serve it to dinner guests warm over vanilla ice cream topped with walnuts. I serve this frequently as a simple and quick dessert during the winter months, and no one ever guesses that I spent the day sewing rather than cooking!

VANILLA ICE CREAM WITH VERMONT MAPLE SYRUP

4 cups vanilla ice cream
1 cup walnuts, shelled and crushed
1½ cups maple syrup

Scoop 1 cup of vanilla ice cream into four small bowls. Sprinkle each with ¼ cup walnuts, and drizzle with warm maple syrup. Serve immediately.

LUCY'S KIMONO

This particular project is a baby kimono made for my new friend Lucy, the daughter of my friends Drew and Kim. Lucy was especially tiny and dear at birth, and when I visited her for the first time in her crib at the hospital, she seemed like a new kitten, stretching, mewing, and blinking her enormous eyes at me. I was completely smitten.

Everyone knows someone like Lucy, and everyone can make this little kimono. It's one of the easiest projects in this book but makes for an impressive gesture at a baby shower or birthday.

Sewing Instructions

❶ Lay Out and Cut Pattern
Trace (see page 149) and cut out the pattern, and then lay out and cut out the pattern pieces as shown in the layout diagram on page 140. Cut 2 Kimono Fronts, 1 Kimono Back, and 2 Sleeves. Use a water-soluble fabric-marking pen to transfer to the cut pieces the pattern markings for placing the ties in the side seams.

❷ Finish Fronts' Short Sides
Fold and press the short side edge of each Kimono Front ⅛" to the wrong side; then fold and press this edge again, this time ¼" to the wrong side. Edge-stitch (see page 155) the top edge of the double fold in place.

❸ Sew Shoulder Seams
With the fabrics' wrong sides together, attach both Kimono Fronts to the Kimono Back at the shoulder seam with a ⅜" seam. Press the shoulder seams open.

❹ Attach Bias Tape to Neckline
Unfold the bias tape, and pin one long edge to the neckline, with the fabrics' right sides together, the raw edges of the neckline and bias tape aligned, and 6" of tape extending beyond each end of the neckline to create ties. Place the pins perpendicular to the tape's edge, so they'll be easy to remove as you sew. Then stitch the tape in place ¼" from the neckline edge, sewing along the tape's fold and removing the pins as you stitch.

Finished Dimensions

Newborn-3 months: chest, 17"; length, 8"

Materials

½ yard of woven fabric

½ yard of contrasting, double-fold, ¼"-wide bias tape

All-purpose thread to match fabric and bias tape

Water-soluble fabric-marking pen

Lucy's Kimono pattern *(see pullout pattern sheet at back of book)*

Choosing Fabric

Make it in shirting or polka-dotted fabric for a baby boy, or a creamy flannel for a wintertime baby. Use one of Dad's old shirts, a vintage pillowcase, or worn linens. This project requires very little fabric—and very little time.

Fold the bias tape over the neckline edge, and press and pin the tape in place on the wrong side. Clean-finish the end of each tie by folding and pressing it, as shown in the drawing at right. Then edge-stitch the tape tie extending from one end of the neckline; "stitch-in-the-ditch"—that is, sew in the seam line made by stitching the binding's first fold—around the neckline to catch the tape's other side, removing the pins as you go; and continue sewing, edge-stitching to the end of the tie at the other end of the neckline. Backstitch (see page 153) at the beginning and end of the seam.

⑤ Sew Sleeves to Body

Match the center of the right Sleeve to the kimono's right shoulder seam, with the fabrics' right sides facing. Sew the Sleeve to the body with a ⅜" seam, and press the seam open. Repeat the process with the left Sleeve.

⑥ Sew Side Seams

Make ties to insert in side seams: Make two 8"-long ties from the remaining bias tape by pressing, edge-stitching, and cutting the tape in half, clean-finishing one end of each tie as you did in Step 4.

Sew side seams: Begin by aligning the Kimono Fronts and Back with right sides together and matching the side edges. Pin the side and underarm seams, inserting the unfinished end of one sewn tie into each side seam at the tie-placement mark you transferred from the pattern ½" below the bottom of the Sleeve (make sure that the ties themselves with their clean-finished end extend on the right side of the Kimono Front and Back in your sewing set-up, as shown in the drawing at right). Sew the side and underarm seams together with a ⅜" seam, backstitching at the beginning and end of the seams. Press the seams to one side (see page 155).

⑦ Hem Sleeves

With the kimono still wrong side out, fold and press one sleeve's edge ⅛" to the wrong side; then fold and press this edge again to the wrong side, this time ¼". Edge-stitch the top edge of the double fold in place. Repeat the process with the other sleeve.

⑧ Hem Bottom Edge

Hem the kimono's bottom edge by turning and pressing it ⅛" to the wrong side, then turning and pressing it again, this time ¼" to the wrong side. Edge-stitch the top edge of the double fold in place.

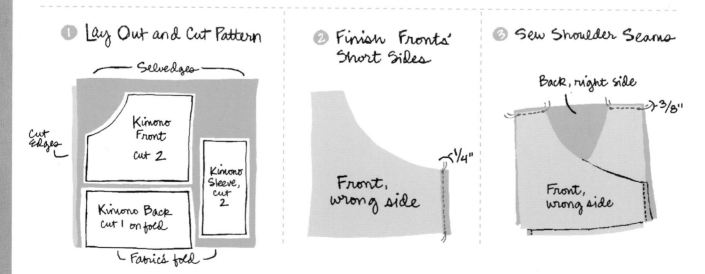

① Lay Out and Cut Pattern
— Selvedges —
Cut Edges
Kimono Front
Cut 2
Kimono Sleeve, cut 2
Kimono Back cut 1 on fold
— Fabrics fold —

② Finish Fronts' Short Sides
¼"
Front, wrong side

③ Sew Shoulder Seams
Back, right side
→3/8"
Front, wrong side

④ Attach Bias Tape to Neckline

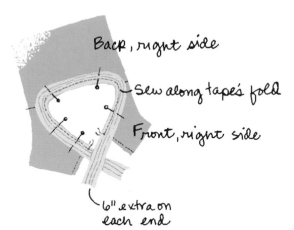

Back, right side

Sew along tape's fold

Front, right side

6" extra on each end

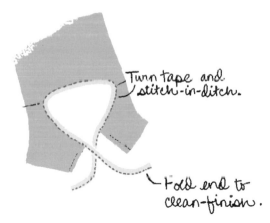

Turn tape and stitch-in-ditch.

Fold end to clean-finish.

Clean-finish ends of bias tape.

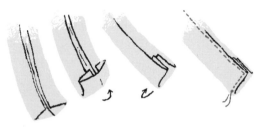

⑤ Sew Sleeves to Body

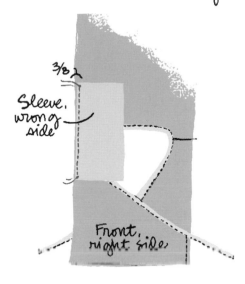

3/8

Sleeve, wrong side

Front, right side

6-7 Sew Side Seams and Hem Sleeves

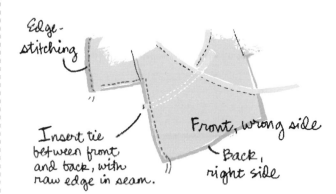

Edge-stitching

Insert tie between front and back, with raw edge in seam.

Front, wrong side

Back, right side

Chapter 4
SEWING BASICS

I started to sew at such a young age that it almost feels like second nature to me. But many of my students are learning for the first time as adults or think they need a refresher course after picking up some elementary skills when they were younger. Either way, I always stress how easy sewing is to learn if you just take it one step at a time.

Choosing a Machine

The most important tool you will choose when starting to sew is a sewing machine. Basically, you have three options: mechanical, electronic, and basic computerized. More complicated computerized machines are also available, but they're meant for specialized tasks like machine embroidery and advanced machine quilting.

A *mechanical machine* is an electrically powered sewing machine with adjustable levers and knobs for selecting tension, stitch length and width, and for making buttonholes and decorative stitches. New machines sell for as little as $100; a used, but well-maintained machine can cost as little as $75 plus $25-50 for servicing if it hasn't been used for more than a year.

An *electronic machine* depends on electronic sensors to determine and adjust settings, which means it can create more precise stitches than a mechanical machine. Instead of levers and knobs, the machine has buttons, sometimes with LCD screens, for changing stitch settings. Prices for a well-made electronic machine start at a few hundred dollars.

A *basic computerized machine* depends on a small microprocessor to control settings as well as complicated graphics for creating embroidery and elaborate stitch patterns. These practically maintenance-free machines are designed for the home sewer who quilts, monograms, and embroiders, and start at around a thousand dollars.

When shopping for a new or used sewing machine, look for one with the following features: a straight stitch, zig-zag stitch, adjustable stitch-length and -width settings, variable-speed function, and buttonhole function. When buying a used machine, look for one that has been well

TEST-DRIVING A MACHINE

Whether you're buying a new or used machine, it's always a good idea to "test-drive" a few models—that is, sew on each machine with an assortment of scrap fabrics to get a feel for how it works. (Take a variety of scraps with you when comparison-shopping, including heavy- and lightweight fabrics, slippery silk, and a knit or jersey.) Here are some questions to ask yourself when test-driving:

- Is this machine easy to thread?
- Does the bobbin wind evenly and smoothly?
- Does the machine sew without vibrating or shaking?
- Does it produce beautiful, straight, even stitches?
- Can you change the stitch speed?
- Are the options for stitch-length and -width settings plentiful or limited?
- Does the machine sew straight lines and curves easily?
- Does the machine sew quietly?
- Does the machine come with a variety of presser feet?
- Is the manual easy to understand?

cared for and comes with a variety of presser feet—I use the buttonhole foot and zipper foot most often—and with an original manual (or at least a threading diagram). If the machine you're interested in doesn't come with its manual, look for one online (try www.sewingmachinemanuals.com).

If you're entirely new to sewing and feel uncomfortable test-driving a machine, ask the salesperson for help. Ask to see how the machine threads (if the threading operation is too convoluted, it won't get any easier once you've got the machine home!) and how the basic stitch settings are adjusted. Ask to see the various attachments and presser feet, and how each one works. Tell the salesperson what you want to eventually sew, whether clothing, quilts, curtains, or bedding, which will help him or her guide you.

And keep in mind that if a machine's small moving parts are made of plastic, they may wear quickly and become misshapen, causing myriad problems. It's best to look for a machine with metal parts along its threading path and in its bobbin casing, even if the machine body is made of plastic. These machines may weigh a bit more than those with plastic moving parts, but they are well worth their heft.

Comparing and Buying New

Fabric and sewing stores are a great place to start learning about sewing machines, especially stores that allow you to test-drive machines you're considering buying. Large fabric-store chains sell a variety of brands at varying prices, and most have websites listing locations nationwide.

There is also a growing number of online stores specializing in sewing machines. Sites like www.allbrands.com and www.sewingmachinesplus.com allow you to easily compare machines, though, of course, not test-drive them.

For sewing-machine reviews and consumer information, look at *Threads* magazine, sold on many magazine racks and online at www.threadsmagazine.com, and at *Consumer Reports*, whose vast archives are online at www.consumerreports.org.

RIGHT I made all of the projects in this book with my trusty, mechanical Necchi Sylvia Maximatic, which is about as old as I am.

Comparing and Buying Used or Vintage

Many used and most vintage sewing machines for sale today are mechanical and, depending on their make and model, have fewer stitch options than their modern counterparts. Still, vintage sewing machines are in high demand and well loved by many home sewers (the Singer Featherweight, introduced in 1933 at the Chicago World Fair, remains the most popular sewing machine in history and is still sought after today).

Many dealers and sewing-machine repair stores understand the value of older machines and will restore and resell quality used machines at great prices, often with a limited warranty. There are also some good online sources for vintage or used machines in good working order, such as www.sewingmachine221sale.com, www.vintagesingersewing.com, www.sewmuse.co.uk, and www.sew-rite.com.

As well, there are numerous online auctions on eBay for used and vintage sewing machines at good prices, which may or may not require some basic repairs. Or you can pursue local sellers, like those on craigslist.org, who may allow you to test-drive their machines before buying.

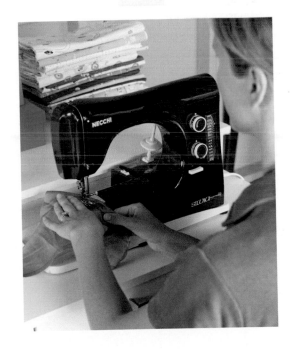

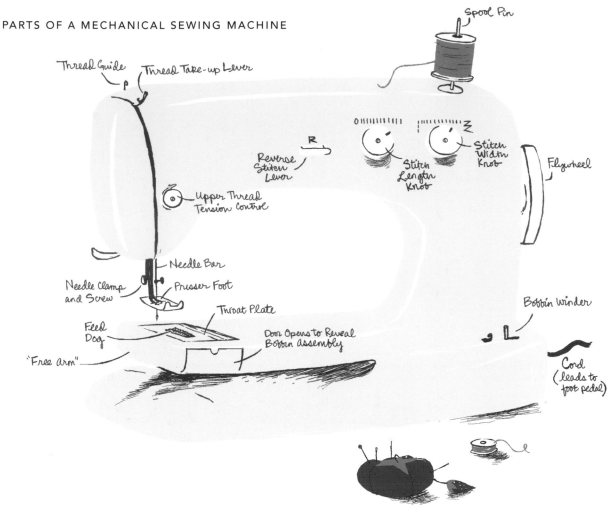

Spool Pin

Thread Guide   Thread Take-up Lever

Reverse
Stitch
Lever

R

Stitch
Length
Knob

Stitch
Width
Knob

Flywheel

Upper Thread
Tension Control

Needle Bar

Needle Clamp
and Screw   Presser Foot

Throat Plate

Feed
Dog

Door Opens to Reveal
Bobbin assembly

"Free arm"

Bobbin Winder

Cord
(leads to
foot pedal)

Learning to Use Your New Machine

Once you have bought a machine, refer to its manual to learn how to it set up. Learning to thread it properly is key: Every home-sewing machine uses a variation of the same basic threading system, but each one is slightly different. When my machine is not stitching well, I immediately check to see that both the bobbin thread and needle thread are properly set, which usually accounts for the problem. For an excellent animated display of how a sewing machine works, check out www.howstuffworks.com/sewing-machine1.htm (look at the bottom, lock-stitch animation); once you see what a delicate balance the machine's many tiny components must maintain, you'll understand why learning to thread your machine properly is so important.

After you've mastered threading your machine and wound a few bobbins, learn to use the tension settings: Use different colors for your bobbin thread and needle thread, and stitch a few inches. Can you see your bobbin thread coming through on the side you are stitching? If so, the needle thread tension is too tight, or the bobbin tension is too loose. If, instead, you can see the needle thread on the bottom layer of fabric, the needle thread is too loose, or the bobbin tension is too tight. When the tension is properly adjusted, the two threads will make a tiny knot between the two fabric layers. Also experiment with zigzag stitches and stitch width, and try sewing a few practice buttonholes (see page 156).

Choosing Fabric

Understanding how different types of fabrics perform is an important part of learning to sew. While the best lessons will come from actual experience, what follows will help you walk the aisles of your local fabric store with confidence.

Almost every fabric, regardless of its fiber content or weight, falls into one of two basic categories based on how it's constructed: woven or knit. A woven fabric is made on a loom from threads that run vertically and horizontally (called the warp and the weft threads, respectively), which are traditionally woven under and over each other. A knit fabric is made on an industrial knitting machine, generally from a single, continuously looped, or knitted, thread, in much the same way as a sweater is knitted by hand. Both woven and knitted fabrics can be suitable for many different types of garments, depending on several key characteristics of the fabric: its *drape*, *body*, *weight*, and *stretch*, or *give*.

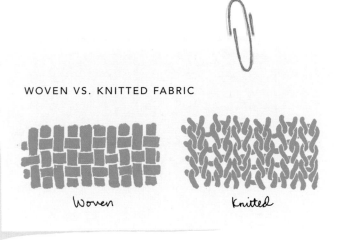

WOVEN VS. KNITTED FABRIC

Woven   Knitted

Fabric with Drape vs. Body

My friend couture tailor Jean Kormos, of Ghost Tailor in New York City, likes to tell her clients that a fabric has either drape or body, but not both. When you remember this rule, choosing fabric for a project becomes a lot easier.

Fabric with drape is meant to move around and lie against your body, creating a silhouette determined by your own shape. When designed and sewn with skill, fabrics that drape can accentuate some curves while disguising others. Think of the dress that Marilyn Monroe wore standing over the subway grate in that iconic scene from *The Seven Year Itch*. When her skirt filled with air, you could see that it was made of yards and yards of fabric; but when she stepped off the grate, the skirt fell against her hips and hung straight down, creating wonderful curving lines at the hem. Fabrics with drape include silk or synthetic jersey, silk charmeuse, and silk crepe.

By contrast, fabric with body creates a silhouette of its own, depending on how it is cut and sewn. Think of A-line coats that stand away from the body or the short shift dresses from the 1960s that stood away from the hips and bust, rather than curving around them. Fabrics with body

DRAPE VS. BODY

Fabric with drape   Fabric with body

garment with drape   garment with body

are especially good for creating crisp silhouettes with volume that don't depend on the body itself for their shape.

Fabrics do not necessarily have to be lightweight to drape; some very heavy silks and synthetics have wonderful drape. And, conversely, some very lightweight fabrics, like stiff cotton voile or silk organza, have tremendous body.

When contemplating the suitability of a fabric at the store, I unwrap a few yards from the bolt, wrap the fabric around my waist, and push out one hip to see how the fabric falls and drapes. This gets some funny looks, but most retailers understand the logic.

Fabric Weight

The weight of the yarn or thread used to make a fabric dramatically affects the finished product. Most fabrics are manufactured with a specific use in mind and are generally classified by their weight: So-called fashion-weight fabrics are suitable for clothing and range from silky blouse fabrics and cotton shirtings to heavier woven fabrics that are also called bottom-weight fabrics because they are intended for skirts and pants. Suiting-weight fabrics are designed for suits, skirts, jackets, and trousers. And décor-weight fabrics include heavier upholstery and drapery fabrics, as well as heavy linens and canvases. At right is a list of my favorite fabrics.

Stretch vs. Non-Stretch Fabric

In addition to drape and body, there are two other basic fabric categories: fabric with or without stretch. Any fabric—whether it has drape or body—can be manufactured with stretch. And nowadays many traditionally nonstretch fabrics are made with added Lycra or spandex, which are essentially miniscule rubber threads that run through one or both directions of the weave or that are worked into the knit.

Regardless of the kind of sewing machine you have, there is one basic rule for sewing with knits: Since the fabric stretches, the seams must also be able to stretch, or they will pop and break. There are two ways to create seams that stretch: For a long, relatively straight seam, simply adjust the stitch to a longer length—3.5-4.5mm, or 7-9 stitches per inch. Then gently stretch your fabric as you

sew. Once the fabric is released and un-stretched, the stitches will be closer together and slightly loose, allowing the seam to stretch again if the fabric is stretched. For complex seams that are not straight and cannot be stretched easily, like those on the Quick Garden Gloves on page 54, use a very narrow zigzag stitch. When the fabric is stretched, the zigzag stitches will stretch out straight. Also key to sewing with knits is using a ball-point needle and polyester thread (see page 151).

Preparing Fabric for Sewing

When sewing, it's crucial to work with fabric that's "square." That means, in the case of woven fabric, that the vertical warp threads run at a true 90 degree angle to the horizontal weft threads—just as the fabric was originally woven on the loom. Likewise in the case of a knit fabric, the knitted loops need to line up correctly as they were originally formed when manufactured. But sometimes, regardless of whether the fabric is woven or knitted, later steps in the manufacturing process (like stretching the fabric for printing or just incorrectly winding the finished fabric on the bolt) may cause what was originally square fabric to get out of square. As a result, unless you square up the fabric

FABRIC CUT SQUARE AND OFF-SQUARE

Edge cut on cross-grain

Edge not cut on cross-grain

Selvedge

Selvedge

FABRICS I LOVE

Below is a small sampling of the vast array of fabrics in the marketplace. These are my favorite fashion- and décor-weight options—and, not surprisingly, the fabrics called for in the projects in this book. I encourage you to find fabrics you like the look and feel of, then to experiment with them as much as possible.

Canvas

- Medium-weight cotton weave
- Smooth finish; plenty of body
- Light enough for pants and skirts but durable enough for upholstery

Denim

- Durable twill fabric similar to jeans fabric
- Strong enough for workhorse bags but stylish enough for skirts and jackets
- Most denims will fade over time

Linen

- Made from flax fibers; has natural, almost waxy sheen
- Uneven weave linens are perfect for summer garments, simple kitchen towels, or pillowcases
- Can be machine-washed and -dried but needs pressing

Quilting cotton

- Lightweight woven cotton, widely available in innumerable colors, weaves, and prints
- Designed to stand up to many washings; perfect for bedding, table linens, and garments

Cotton Lawn

- Very lightweight woven cotton, often printed with delicate florals
- Favored for elegant but simple featherweight garments
- Fabric's look and feel improves with every machine-washing

Shirting

- Lightweight woven, made from fine, soft cotton or silk yarns
- Originally developed for men's dress shirts but also perfect for dresses, blouses, and curtains
- Often woven with different colored yarns to produce stripes, checks, and plaids
- Can usually be machine-washed and -dried, but delicate versions may need hand-washing

Silk Jersey

- Beautiful, versatile silk knit that drapes beautifully
- Virtually wrinkle-free; can be tossed into washer and dryer
- Elegant, practical, and stylish fabric for dresses and skirts

Wool Melton or Blanket Wool

- Very tightly woven wool that is brushed or felted to create smooth finish
- Extremely warm and soft; perfect for heavy coats, blankets, and cushions
- Can be shrunk and thickened by machine-washing in hot water before using; but once desired weight is achieved, must be hand-washed, or it will continue to shrink

again before sewing it and unless you position your pattern pieces correctly with the straight (squared) grain of the fabric, your garment will also be out of square.

Ask the salesperson to cut the yardage either by tearing it (meaning to actually rip it across its width, which gives you a very straight edge since the rip follows a cross-wise weft thread in the fabric's weave) or by "pulling a thread" (meaning to pull out a single weft thread, leaving a tiny, but visible empty space in the fabric's weave to serve as a cutting guide). Both cutting methods will give you a square cut, even if sometimes the cut fabric still looks out of square. But square fabric that just looks out of square is easily remedied by "trueing" it.

Trueing Your Fabric

The process of trueing woven fabric involves washing, drying, and pressing it to make sure that all its horizontal and vertical threads line up perfectly, as they did when the fabric was originally woven. Trueing the fabric returns it to its original square state and should always be done before cutting pattern pieces from it. An added benefit of trueing is that it preshrinks the fabric. (Before you start trueing your fabric, if it was *not* cut correctly at the fabric store by either ripping it on the cross-grain or pulling a cross-grain thread, as explained above, do this now yourself on both of the fabric's cut ends.)

To true your fabric, first machine-wash it in warm water with a gentle detergent; then machine-dry it on medium heat. Press the washed and dried fabric if wrinkled, lay the fabric flat, and smooth it from the center towards the selvedges and cut edges. Next fold the fabric across its width, and smooth it out until its cut edges match (the cut edges will match exactly only if your fabric was torn or cut on the straight grain), as shown in the drawing at top right. Put a few pins into the fabric to keep the folded layers from slipping, and press the squared fabric again, so it's ready for cutting out the pattern pieces.

While trueing the fabric may seem like a lot of work, it makes a world of difference in the way your finished project looks and feels.

TRUEING FABRIC

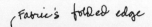

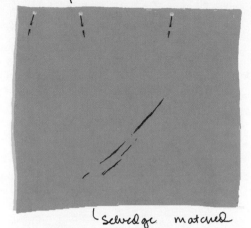

Fabric's folded edge

Selvedge matched

Fold fabric width-wise, match cut edges and selvedges, and pin fold.

Smooth fabric away from folded edge until both cut edges, match, and press fabric again.

Transferring Pattern onto Fabric

Traditionally, sewers cut a pattern out of pattern paper, pin the cut pattern pieces on the fabric, and cut around the pattern pieces to cut the fabric out. I prefer to trace the original pattern in the size I want, and then transfer the pattern pieces from the tracing onto the fabric, which preserves the original pattern in all sizes.

For the trace-and-transfer method, I use a handy type of tracing paper coated on one side with a fine marking powder (each sheet can be re-used many times) and a tool called a tracing wheel. To use transfer paper, first fold the fabric if your project's cutting diagram calls for folding. Next, lay the tracing paper, coated side down, on the fabric. Then cut apart the traced pattern pieces (you don't need to cut out each piece exactly on its edges; just cut around the pieces to separate them since you'll be tracing the pattern piece's outlined edges onto the fabric), and lay them out on your fabric.

Laying Out and Tracing Pattern

When laying out pattern pieces on fabric to trace them, it's key to line up the pattern pieces with the fabric's straight grain. To help you do this, most patterns have a grain line arrow printed on them, and aligning the pattern with the fabric's straight grain simply involves making sure the pattern's grain line arrow runs parallel to the fabric's selvedge edges, as shown in the drawing at right. (Occasionally a pattern will call for aligning the pattern pieces with the fabric's bias—that is, at a 45-degree angle to the straight grain—but, in those cases, the project's layout diagram will show you how to position the pattern pieces.) And if the pattern piece notes that one of its edges should be "cut on the fold," place that edge on the fabric's fold.

After laying out the pattern pieces on the tracing paper and fabric, use beanbags or small weights to hold down the fabric layers and prevent them from shifting. Then use the tracing wheel to carefully trace the outline of each pattern piece, transferring marks that produce a marked line on the fabric.

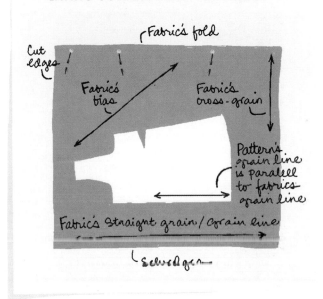

LAYING OUT AND TRACING PATTERN

Cutting Out Pattern

After marking the fabric, remove the pattern pieces (but replace the weights to hold the fabric layers together), and cut out your fabric following the traced lines. Many home sewers (and especially quilters) now use a rotary cutter and a self-healing cutting mat (see page 150) to cut out patterns, which saves time and produces straight, even edges. Because the fabric is not lifted from the table, as it is when cut with shears, it does not shift as easily. And cutting with a rotary blade enables you to make a series of continuous cuts, rather than the stop-and-go action involved in using shears.

If you want to use traditional sewing shears instead of a rotary cutter, be sure the shears are sharp. It's also a good idea to pin the fabric layers together at the center of each pattern piece, so the bottom layer does not shift. Finally, after cutting out the pattern pieces, regardless of the tool used, label and transfer any pattern markings onto the cut pattern pieces with a water-soluble fabric-marking pen.

Tools You'll Need

At first glance, a retailer's wall of sewing tools can be overwhelming: hundreds of tiny packages with mysterious labels and contents. Do not panic. Project by project, your toolkit will grow, and soon you'll be debating the pros and cons of tailor's chalk and point turners with the best of them. To get started, below is a list of tools needed to complete basic projects (like those in this book).

Measuring and Marking Tools

MEASURING TAPE
I like a retractable 60" or longer tape marked in both centimeters and inches since many patterns in our global crafting community bear metric measurements.

TRANSPARENT RULER
A wide, thick, transparent ruler marked with a grid enables you to make lines parallel to your fabric's edge. It can also serve as a cutting guide with a rotary cutter, and its grid lines can be used to find right angles accurately.

WATER-SOLUBLE FABRIC-MARKING PEN
These markers are wonderful to use on light-colored fabric since their lines disappear when pressed with a steam iron (for marks that survive pressing, use a fabric pen whose marks only come out with washing). Use marking pens to transfer pattern markings like button and buttonhole placements, pockets, and darts.

TAILOR'S CHALK
This traditional, inexpensive tool makes marks on fabric that can be removed after sewing. The chalk's square shape makes it easy to draw straight lines, and it does not need sharpening like a chalk pencil. It is especially useful for dark, heavy fabrics on which the dark lines of a traditional water-soluble marking pen may not be visible.

CHALK PENCIL
This is a pencil filled with chalk, not lead, with a brush at one end to remove chalk marks.

Cutting Tools

ROTARY CUTTER AND CUTTING MAT
Configured like a pizza cutter, a rotary cutter works especially well for cutting knits and slippery and fine fabrics that can shift around when cut with scissors. Rotary cutters come in various sizes; the smaller the blade, the easier it cuts around corners and curves. Be very careful with a rotary cutter since you can cut yourself badly if you're careless.

You'll also need disposable rotary blades and a cutting mat to protect your cutting surface. There are two basic types of cutting mats—self-healing (whose surface absorbs the blade's cuts and remains unscarred) and non-self-healing—and both are sold with and without gridded ruler lines. I recommend a gridded, self-healing mat, as large as you can make space for.

SHEARS
Heavy-duty sewing shears made entirely of steel will last a lifetime if cared for properly. Keeping scissors sharp is very important, and the best way to do so is to only use them with fabric (never paper and plastic!). Some sewing stores offer scissor sharpening services.

THREAD SNIPS
Shaped like an elongated, curved U with blades on either end, thread snips are a great tool for trimming threads quickly as you work, so clean-up at a project's end is minimal.

PINKING SHEARS
These scissors have sawtooth edges designed to trim the raw, straight edges of fabrics to prevent fraying, and curved edges to allow them to spread out and lie flat. Pinking-shear blades cannot be sharpened easily. Since they dull quickly, choose the least expensive pair you can find.

SEAM RIPPER
This tool is used to rip out an incorrectly sewn seam or to cut up the center line of a buttonhole. A seam ripper has two points, a dull one for reaching under threads without piercing the fabric and a narrow, sharp one for sliding between the fabric layers making up a seam. When the sharp, curved edge between the points begins to dull, replace it. A dull seam ripper creates more problems than it solves.

Sewing Tools

MACHINE-SEWING NEEDLES

There are many types of needles for home-sewing machines, each designed for use with a different fabric or for a special task, but you will only need four needles for the projects in this book: a universal needle, a ball-point needle, a leather needle, and a microtex/sharp needle.

A universal needle works best on medium-weight woven fabrics, and I try to always have medium-sized (size 10 or 12) universals on hand. For sewing knit and stretch fabrics, use a ball-point needle, whose rounded tip slides easily between the fabric's threads rather than piercing or snagging them. When sewing on very fine fabrics like silk, gauze, or velvet, use a microtex/sharp needle, which has a very fine, extremely sharp point.

It is important to replace needles frequently. A needle that is even slightly bent or dull can create a lot of problems, like skipped or uneven stitches, and will require your machine's motor to work harder, thus shortening its life.

HAND-SEWING NEEDLES

Like machine-sewing needles, hand-sewing needles come in a wide range of types for various tasks, so it's a good idea to keep an assortment package on hand. For the projects in this book, you will need what's called a sharp needle and an embroidery needle. A sharp needle is used for most types of hand-sewing, including hemming and finishing work. An embroidery needle is a long, strong needle with an elongated eye to accommodate embroidery and other decorative threads and is used for, yes, embroidery and decorative stitching.

THREAD

Thread comes in many varieties, and it's a good idea to pair your fabric with the thread that best works with it. When buying fabric, hold your selections up to the thread rack to find matching spools and buy them right along with the fabric, even if you don't plan to use the fabric until much later.

For sewing woven cotton and linen, use *cotton thread*. Since these fabrics crease easily, they often need pressing with a very hot iron; and cotton thread is heat-resistant

and will stand up to frequent pressing. But don't use cotton thread on cotton or linen knits and stretchy fabrics because these stitches will break when the fabric is stretched. Instead, sew all knits and stretchy fabric with *all-purpose polyester thread*, which can actually be used with almost all fabrics. Polyester thread is stronger than cotton thread and has a little give to it and a fine coating of wax or silicone to help it move through the fabric easily. Be careful, though, when ironing polyester thread, since a very hot iron can weaken it; use low to medium heat with it. Another excellent all-purpose thread is *cotton-wrapped polyester thread*, which has the strength of polyester and the heat-resistance of cotton; it can also be used with knits (though I prefer all-purpose polyester thread for knits).

For sewing silk or wool, I use *silk thread*, a thin, smooth thread with a lovely sheen. I also use silk thread for hand-basting stitches, because it can be pulled out of the fabric without leaving any marks or holes, and as well for adding decorative stitches or hand-sewing a hem.

Several projects in this book call for *elastic thread* to create stretchy rows of smocking. Elastic thread is made from a stretchy polyurethane thread wrapped in a coil of polyester threads, which uncoils when the polyurethane is stretched. Use elastic thread only in your bobbin, and wrap the bobbin by hand rather than using the machine's bobbin winder. Long sold only in white or black, elastic thread is now available in a wide range of colors, thanks to a recently introduced high-quality line from Gütermann. See page 155 for information on "Sewing with Elastic Thread."

NEEDLE THREADER

Nothing more than a thin wire loop with a handle, a needle threader is handy for threading both hand-sewing and machine needles. To use a needle threader, push its wire loop through the needle's eye, insert thread into the loop, and pull the loop back out of the needle's eye. That's it!

THIMBLE

Protect your fingertips when hand-sewing with a standard metal thimble. The indentations on a thimble's surface can be used to anchor the back of your needle and force it through even the thickest layers of fabric. Thimbles come in various sizes, and you'll need to try out a size or two to find one that's comfortable. It will feel awkward at first, but eventually you will come to rely on it. There are also leather thimbles, which are like wearing a protective second skin that allows you to retain some sensitivity in your fingertip.

PINCUSHION
A pincushion is a must for keeping pins handy. There are many styles of pincushions. I'm a fan of the traditional tomato-shaped pincushion because, unlike most pincushions, it holds a little known secret: The tiny strawberry anchored to its side is filled with emery, which will sharpen the needles and pins you push into it.

IRON
Although at first glance, an iron may not seem like a sewing tool, per se, it's a tool that you'll use throughout the construction process to press folds, flatten or shape edges, turn under hems, press seam allowances, and so on. You will want a sturdy iron that has a large steam reservoir and produces a good, misting spray. After owning (and dropping, thus rendering leaky and unstable) several fancy, lightweight plastic irons, I was thrilled to learn about Black and Decker's newly updated The Classic Iron (# F63E), which is modeled after the same iron that my grandmother used to press her table linens. This is a simple, inexpensive iron with a heavy metal base that gets insanely hot, works quickly and beautifully, and will last forever.

Miscellaneous Tools

BUTTONHOLE FOOT
To make a buttonhole on most machines, you'll need to replace the machine's standard presser foot with a buttonhole foot. When attached, the buttonhole foot has a small ruler that runs on both sides of the needle, enabling you to make a buttonhole precisely as long as you want it. This foot comes with most machines, but if you've bought a used machine, you may need to buy one from your machine dealer or from an online source. For information on sewing a buttonhole, see page 156.

POINT TURNER
A point turner is a simple, shaped piece of wood or plastic to help fully push out a corner or a straight or curved seam when turning a sewn piece right side out. Using a point turner is utterly simple: Position the turner's point in the corner or spot that needs turning out, and gently push and work the spot until it's completely turned out. Then "finger-press" the area before pressing it with your iron.

LOOP TURNER
Nothing more than a long piece of sturdy wire with a hook at one end and a small handle on the other, a loop turner is used to turn right side out a narrow sewn tube of fabric, like a spaghetti strap. To use a loop turner, insert it through the fabric tube, catch the hook in the far end of the tube's seam and seam allowances, and begin pulling the turner toward you, working the tube right side out as you pull.

FUSIBLE HEM TAPE
Fusible hem tape is a narrow strip of double-sided fusible interfacing, usually sold in small rolls, that is used to fuse two layers of fabric together by sandwiching the layers around the tape and pressing the trio with a hot iron. Typically, these tapes are used to hold a hem in place temporarily while you sew it, but there are some tapes on the market that manufacturers claim to be permanent, even through machine-washing and -drying.

BIAS TAPE MAKER
A bias tape maker is used to make folded bias tape from strips of fabric cut on the bias, or diagonal. A strip of fabric is pushed into one end and emerges from the other having been forced into a fold, ready to be pressed. Bias tape makers are available in many sizes, and are typically used in conjunction with a hot steam iron.

NOTEBOOK
I use a notebook to keep track of seam allowances, pattern changes, and general ideas, and to hold pictures, magazine clippings, and fabric swatches.

Sewing Techniques

Learning to use a sewing machine can be a little challenging at first since it involves using both hands and one foot—remember learning to drive a car or ride a bike? Give yourself lots of time to practice on different types of fabric with different types of stitches, and be patient!

Stitches You'll Need

Below is a glossary of stitches you'll need for the projects in this book. On page 154 are illustrations of all of them. Unless otherwise noted, these stitches are machine stitches, not hand stitches.

STRAIGHT STITCH

A straight stitch is the stitch most commonly used in sewing, for example, when sewing seams, topstitching, and edge stitching. On most sewing machines, you can adjust the stitch's length; and although most sewing calls for a regular stitch length (2.5-3 mm, or 10-12 stitches per inch for mid-weight fabrics), some project directions will call for a shorter or longer stitch length. All the machine stitches explained below are variations on the straight stitch.

When hand-sewing a straight stitch (also called a running stitch), be careful to keep both your stitches and the spaces between them the same consistent length, typically ⅛" to ¼" long. Also make sure to always sew with the same tension, so your stitches lie flat rather than bunching up along the stitching line.

ZIGZAG STITCH

Most home-sewing machines made in the last fifty years feature a stitch-width adjustment lever. By adjusting the stitch's width, you can make your needle move to the right and left as it sews, either subtly or dramatically, depending on how wide and long you set the stitch to be. This stitch is aptly named the zigzag stitch. Unlike a straight stitch, a zigzag stitch, even a very narrow one, has some give to it—that is, it stretches a little when pulled from end to end. Thus, a zigzag stitch is the stitch of choice for sewing knits and other stretch fabrics, and also when sewing a waist seam or sleeve hem. (See another way to make stitches that stretch on page 146 and information on sewing with elastic thread on page 155.)

BASTING STITCH

Basting stitches are long, loose, easy-to-remove straight stitches used to temporarily join layers of fabric. Most commonly sewn by hand, basting stitches can also be sewn by machine by setting your stitch length to its longest setting (about 4mm or 6 stitches per inch). Basting stitches are used for various reasons, including to hold a curved or complex shape, like a collar or shoulder, in place—much as pins do—while you machine-sew the seam with more permanent stitches. Basting stitches can also be used to gather fabric.

To baste by hand, thread a hand-sewing needle with a single strand of silk thread (see page 151) and tie a knot in one end. Then sew a series of long, straight running stitches (see the drawing on page 153) along the edge you want to baste.

If you want to gather with basting stitches, start by sewing two rows of basting stitches ⅛" to ¼" apart along the edge to be gathered. Then remove the needle from your thread, and carefully pull the thread while pushing the fabric towards the thread's knotted end, as though you are removing the wrapper from a straw. Distribute the gathers evenly along the gathered width you need, and wrap the thread tail in a figure-8 around a pin to secure the gathered edge temporarily. Use an iron to press the gathers flat, and machine-stitch, using a regular straight stitch, just above the basting stitches (not through them) to secure the gathers. Cut off the knotted end(s) of the basting thread, and pull the thread to remove it.

BACKSTITCH AND LOCKSTITCH

Backstitching is one way to secure the beginning and end of a row of stitching to keep the stitches from raveling. Alternatively you can lockstitch or tie off your threads (see page 155). To backstitch (or "back-tack") at the beginning of a row of stitches, position the needle a couple stitches ahead of where you want to start stitching. Then use the machine's reverse button to stitch backwards to the point where you want the stitching line to start, release the reverse button, and start stitching forward as you normally would. At the end of your stitching line, again push the machine's reverse button, and sew a couple stitches in reverse over the last few stitches of your stitching line.

STITCH GLOSSARY

Straight Stitch
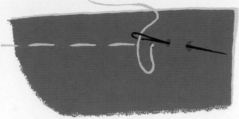

Zigzag Stitch
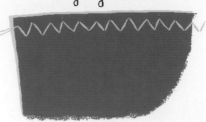

Basting Stitch
(used here for gathering)

2 rows ⅛" to ¼" apart

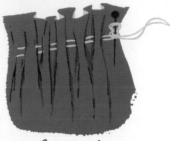
Secure with
figure-8 around pin

Backstitch

Lockstitch
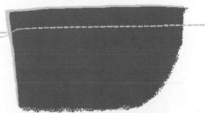

Topstitch

Edge-stitch

Lockstitching is an easy, elegant, and essentially invisible way to secure a seam or any line of stitching, and it's the preferred method for securing smocking sewn with elastic thread. To lockstitch at the beginning of a seam, set the stitch length to zero (or near zero) and take a couple of stitches in place; then reset the stitch length to its regular setting, and sew as you normally would. At the end of the seam, repeat the process. Finally, pull the top thread to the fabric's wrong side, and knot off with the bobbin thread.

Perhaps the cleanest way to finish off a line of stitches, both at the beginning and end of the stitching, is to tie off the bobbin and needle threads together. If your seam or stitching begins and ends at the edge of your fabric, tying off the two threads is an easy matter of double-knotting them with a square knot. If the seam or stitching line ends away from the fabric's edge and the threads cannot easily reach one another, use a hand-sewing needle to stitch the top (needle) thread through your fabric to the fabric's wrong side, and tie it off tightly with the bobbin thread.

TOPSTITCH AND EDGE-STITCH

Topstitching and edge-stitching both involve straight-stitching (see page 153) and are used mainly to finish and reinforce an edge but can also provide a decorative touch. The chief difference between topstitching and edge-stitching is the distance at which the stitches are sewn from the edge: As its name suggests, edge-stitches are sewn very close to a folded or sewn edge, usually 1/16" to 1/8" away. Topstitching sits more than 1/8" from the edge and could be any distance from 1/4" to several inches or even more from that edge. Other than the distance from the edge, there is very little difference between the two.

Several projects in this book use topstitching to finish and reinforce seams. To topstitch a seam, begin by pressing the seam on the wrong side, pressing both seam allowances to one side of the seam (see right). Then, with the project and seam right side up, sew a line of stitches parallel to the seam line. Typically topstitching is sewn 1/4" from the seam, which catches the seam allowances beneath, assuming the allowances are 3/8" or 1/2" wide (both standard widths).

SLIPSTITCH

A slipstitch is a hand-stitch used to join two edges of fabric almost invisibly. When slipstitching, take very small stitches, picking up just a few threads from one edge and then stitching diagonally into the other edge, again taking only a tiny bit of fabric. Among other uses, a slipstitch can be used to stitch a hand-rolled hem (see page 156).

Pressing Seams Open or to One Side

After sewing a seam, press the seam allowances open (that is, with each allowance pressed in the opposite direction from the seam line itself) or to one side (with both seam allowances pressed together to one side of the seam). A seam pressed open has less bulk than one pressed to one side. Sometimes a seam is pressed to one side, so its allowances can be topstitched to accentuate or strengthen the seam. The project directions will tell you how to press the seam. If they don't, you can leave the seam unpressed, and the seam's bulk will not be an issue in constructing the project.

Sewing with Elastic Thread

By using elastic thread in your bobbin and all-purpose thread as your top, or needle, thread, you can make stitches that stretch (see also *zigzag stitch* at left for another kind of stretch stitch). And if you sew several closely spaced parallel rows of these stretchy stitches with elastic thread, you can create what's called elasticized smocking, which is commonly used on the bodices of women's and girls' sundresses, because it creates a snug, but comfortable fit.

Use elastic thread only in your bobbin, not as your top (needle) thread. To fill a bobbin with elastic thread, gently wind it by hand, without stretching the thread as you wrap it, until the bobbin is full. Load the filled bobbin into your machine as for any bobbin, and use regular thread on top.

Always begin and end rows of elasticized stitching with lockstitching (see above) to help keep the ends secure, or tie off the ends. And always sew with the right side of your project facing up, so the elastic bobbin thread shows on the back, not the front, of the fabric. After sewing one or more rows of elasticized stitches, use a hot steam iron to press the stitches. The elastic will "shrink" when pressed, and the fabric will soften and adapt to its new shape.

Making Spaghetti

Spaghetti (the fabric kind) is a pliable tubular "string" made with fabric using a tool called loop turner (see page 152). Spaghetti can be used for straps on formal and casual dresses, as well as for belts, drawstrings, and other trim.

To make spaghetti with a loop turner, cut a piece of fabric 1" wide and any desired length. Fold the fabric in half, with right sides together; press the folded fabric; and join the layers with a ¼" seam. Insert the loop turner in one end of the sewn tube and push it through the tube until it emerges at the other end. Attach the hook at the top end of the loop turner to the far end of the tube's seam and seam allowances, and begin to carefully pull the loop turner towards you to turn the tube inside out through the tube. After completely turning the tube right side out, roll the spaghetti between your palms to "round" it. When you wash the spaghetti, the seam allowances inside will fluff up, giving the spaghetti even more shape and fullness.

Sewing a Hand-Rolled Hem

When finishing a more formal skirt or dress, working with very fine fabrics, or hemming a curved edge, a delicate hand-rolled hem is best. Thread a needle with a single strand of thread, and make a small knot in the end of one thread. Roll the edge of the fabric tightly between the fingers on one hand as you slipstitch (see the drawing below) the rolled edge with the other hand.

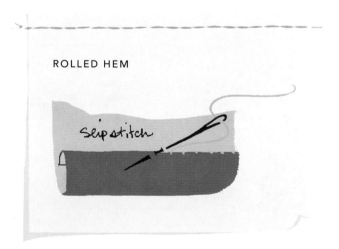

ROLLED HEM

slip stitch

Making Buttonholes

Buttonholes are made by sewing a rectangle of zigzag stitches—two narrow-zigzag vertical "legs," capped top and bottom by a wide-zigzag horizontal bar—to create a reinforced area in the fabric that can be slit to allow a button to pass through.

To make a buttonhole, first determine how large an opening your button needs: Cut a small strip of paper, about 4" long x ¼" wide. Wrap the strip around the button's widest part, grasping the paper firmly where its two edges meet; pencil-mark this point; and remove the button. Keeping the paper strip folded, flatten it, and measure and record the length from fold to pencil mark.

Most patterns have markings (usually an "X") indicating where to place the center of the buttonholes. Transfer these markings onto your cut fabric pattern pieces with a water-soluble fabric-marking pen, then draw a centered vertical line through each X the length of your button measurement.

Attach the buttonhole foot to your machine. This foot has ruled marks on it, so you can measure and sew the exact length needed for your marked buttonhole. Always practice making a few buttonholes on scrap fabric before sewing on your actual garment, and cut one of the practice buttonholes open to make sure it fits your button.

Many machines have automatic buttonhole settings. If yours doesn't, follow the steps below and illustrated at right to manually machine-sew a buttonhole.

❶ Sew Top Horizontal Bar (SETTINGS: *Machine's adjustable needle bar*: center; *stitch length*: just above zero; *stitch width*: widest possible)

Place the fabric under the buttonhole foot, with the needle positioned at the top end of the marked buttonhole line. Sew a few stitches, which will be wide, almost completely horizontal stitches, creating a horizontal "bar" for the top of the buttonhole. Stop stitching at the far left side of the bar, with the needle down in the fabric.

❷ Sew Left Leg (SETTINGS: *Needle bar*: far left; *stitch length*: almost zero; *stitch width*: medium)

Stitch down the marked line to the bottom, stopping at the far left, with the needle down in the fabric.

❸ **Sew Bottom Horizontal Bar** (SETTINGS: *Needle bar:* center; *stitch length:* almost zero; *stitch width:* widest possible)

Sew a few stitches, creating the bottom horizontal bar. Stop stitching at the far right, with the needle down in the fabric.

❹ **Sew Right Leg** (SETTINGS: *Needle bar:* center; *stitch length:* almost zero; *stitch width:* medium)

Sew in reverse back up the buttonhole's length to the beginning stitches.

❺ **Lockstitch to Finish** (SETTING: *Stitch width:* zero)

Secure the buttonhole stitches by lockstitching (see page 153). To open the buttonhole, use a seam ripper, small scissors, or buttonhole cutter to cut the fabric between the two stitching rows, being careful not to cut the stitches themselves.

Sewing on a Button

Sew buttons on by hand with a hand-sewing needle and cotton or poly-cotton thread that matches your button (not the fabric) unless you want to add interest by using a contrasting thread.

❶ Mark your button placements: After cutting your sewn buttonholes open, lay the garment flat, with the buttonhole placket positioned over where you want the buttons to go. Push the tip of a water-soluble fabric marking pen through the center of each open buttonhole, making a small button-placement mark on the fabric beneath. Using a single, knotted strand of thread and working on the right side, make a small stitch in the same spot you marked.

❷ Sew in and out of the holes in the button in an X pattern until the button is secure. Your last stitch should come through the fabric from the back, ending between the button and the fabric's right side.

❸ Then wrap the thread around the sewn thread shank below the button several times, pulling all of the threads together. Push the needle through the shank and knot off several times. Clip thread tails.

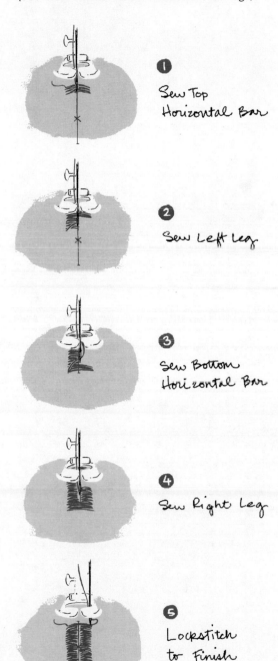

MACHINE-SEWING A BUTTONHOLE
(See main text for needle and stitch settings)

❶ Sew Top Horizontal Bar

❷ Sew Left Leg

❸ Sew Bottom Horizontal Bar

❹ Sew Right Leg

❺ Lockstitch to Finish

RESOURCES

The fabrics and tools mentioned in this book can be found at fabric stores worldwide and through these retailers.

PURL PATCHWORK

147 Sullivan St., New York, NY 10012
212-420-8798   www.purlsoho.com

A great source for all kinds of fabrics (including Liberty of London), plus sewing and quilting supplies, patterns, and books; also offers sewing and quilting classes.

M & J TRIMMING

1008 Sixth Ave.
New York, NY 10018
1-800-9-MJTRIM
www.mjtrim.com

Huge selection of trim, including purse handles, chain, buttons, rickrack, zippers, ribbon, and more. (Hardware for Town Bag, page 64)

VERMONT ORGANIC FIBER COMPANY

www.vtorganicfiber.com

Offers organic, specialty wool fabrics, including wool for Guest-Room Slippers, page 45, and Patchwork-Trimmed Baby Blanket, page 122.

BRETTUNS VILLAGE LEATHER

www.brettunsvillage.com/leather

Offers an assortment of leather and leather trim. (Metallic hide for Town Bag, page 64)

JOANN FABRIC AND CRAFT STORES

Everything the home sewer could want, including fabric, interfacing, elastic thread, and sewing tools, all at great prices! Find a store near you or shop online at www.joann.com.

REPRODEPOTFABRICS.COM

www.reprodepotfabrics.com

Specializes in designer, vintage reproduction, retro, and hard-to-find Japanese fabrics, plus trims. (Carries almost every line of fabric used in this book.)

MOOD FABRICS

225 W 37th St., 3rd Floor   6151 W. Pico Blvd.
New York, NY 10018   Los Angeles, CA 90035
212-730-5003   323-653-MOOD

www.moodfabrics.com

Dizzying array of designer fabrics, including silk jersey for Saturday-Night Silk-Jersey Set, page 90, and leather for Town Bag, page 64.

VINTAGESINGERSEWING.COM

www.vintagesingersewing.com

Multiple brands and types of used and vintage sewing machines and parts, including Featherweight machines.

WEST ELM

www.westelm.com

(Source of Jay Desk on page 8)

MANHATTAN WARDROBE SUPPLY

245 West 29th St., 8th Floor
New York, NY 10001
212-268-9993
www.wardrobesupplies.com

Great source for sewing supplies and hard-to-find items, like colored elastic thread, the sold-out-everywhere Black and Decker Classic Iron, and industrial equipment.

CLOTILDE

www.clotilde.com

Much-loved sewing-supply mail-order catalog serving the home sewer for 35 years and now with an online store. Clotilde is also a good source for tips, demos, and how-to information.

Blogs and Communities

There are so many great blogs and communities on the Internet. These are a few that I check regularly.

angrychicken.typepad.com

designspongeonline.com

greenkitchen.com/blog

homecompanionmag.com

melaniefalickbooks.com

purlbee.com

sewingmamas.com

taunton.com/threads

whipup.net

TIAS.COM

www.tias.com

Huge collection of sewing machine manuals and threading diagrams for vintage machines, as well as machines and parts.

HEARTHSONG

www.hearthsong.com

Sewing and crafts supplies for kids, including miniature sewing machines, sewing kits, and gifts.

FABRIC TEMPTATIONS

942 G St., Arcata, CA 95521
707-822-7782   www.fabtemp.com

Unique fabric store specializing in textiles from around the world, one-of-a-kind items, hard-to-find supplies, organic and handmade items. The knowledgable staff prefers to help folks over the phone (rather than online).

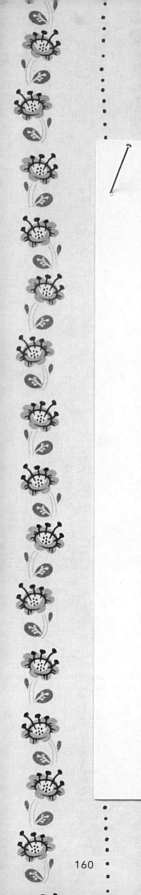

ACKNOWLEDGMENTS

I would like to thank my husband, TC Fleming, for supporting this project wholeheartedly.

Thanks also to Joelle Hoverson at Purl Patchwork in New York City, for introducing me to the world of craft publishing and to the NYC crafting community at large and for providing such a lovely and inspirational space in which to teach and share ideas.

Thanks to the very talented John Gruen, for always being such a joy to work with and for making 7am somehow fun, and to Brooke Hellewell Reynolds, who kept me from eating the cookies that were meant to be used later as props (even though there were PLENTY of extras) and for her hard work on our photo shoots and designing this book. Thanks also to my beautiful models: Jenny McCaffrey and her family, Paisley Gregg, Jessica Cary, Ruby Reynolds, Eva Goldfinger, Calvin Cacciamani, Ben and Chris Whipple, Ann Taylor, Kristen Allore.

Thanks to Kerry Canfield and BJ Graham and to New Pond Farm and Warrups Farm (both near Redding, Connecticut) for supplying such stunning scenery, and to my friends Tim and Susannah at Blueberry Hill Inn in Goshen, Vermont, for allowing us to set up camp in their little paradise for what must have seemed like a very long weekend. Thanks to Gordon Ticehurst in Beacon for sharing his wild little garden. Thanks also to Djerba Goldfinger and her company, Reprodepot.com, for supplying so many beautiful fabrics, and to my friends at Fabric Temptations in Arcata, California, for sharing their expertise and assisting me with the tools section.

Thanks to Denyse Schmidt, my very inspiring friend, for allowing us to use her beautiful studio, and for her eye-opening workshops and lessons shared, professional and personal.

Special thanks to my editor and friend Melanie Falick, who trusted me with this opportunity. Of that I am overly proud. Thanks also to Laura Kadlijek, Bob and Siv Berg, Ellie and Lee Matt, Leeann Myers, Vera McClaughlin, and Michael and Uli Belenky for creative support and inspiration.

And lastly, thanks to Mrs. Grandshaw, my home-economics teacher at Enosburg Falls High School. Mrs. G taught thousands of young women to sew, cook, and manage their homes with thrift, ingenuity, and creativity (and to cross their legs at the ankle, NOT the knee) for over twenty years.

PANTONE®
184 U